"I have known Jason since he was a nineteen-year-old with big dreams. He never gave up on those dreams no matter how tough the going. Now he lives his dream every day. The message in this book will help you do the same."

—Admiral Bob Inman, former director,
National Security Agency, and deputy director, CIA

"Jason Dorsey has beautifully and powerfully captured the essence of the questions that have always been of concern to young adults but seldom addressed in as clear and compelling fashion. Regardless of our age, we make choices each day that have long-lasting effects on our success and fulfillment. *My Reality Check Bounced!* will help readers make wise choices about their futures."

—Robert Goodwin, president and CEO, Points of Light Foundation

"*My Reality Check Bounced!* is a real gem of insight and practicality. This book will be a valued asset to any twentysomething who wants more out of life."

—Dr. Pat Schwallie-Giddis, director of graduate programs in counseling
and human studies, George Washington University

"Jason's book is filled with honest stories about young adults who have searched deep inside to find the happiness they were missing. The practical exercises and timely actions can help anyone create the future they desire."

—Bob Carlquist, former executive vice president
and general manager, *Houston Chronicle*

"If communities tap into the ideas in this book, they will be much better prepared to unleash the talent of their young professionals."

—Angelos Angelou, principal, Angelou Economics

"*My Reality Check Bounced!* delivers concrete action steps and real-world examples that any recent graduate can use immediately to live with more passion and purpose."

—Cal Newport, author of *How to Become a Straight-A Student*
and *How to Win at College*

"Jason hits the bulls-eye in revealing the fears and hopes twentysomethings wake up to each morning. As a peer who "walks his talk," he skillfully cuts through the standard real-world excuses to help twentysomethings figure out who they are and how far they can go. Jason's credible message will inspire you whether you're in your first real job or ten years into your career."

—Mike Sheridan, former executive director, Texas Workforce Commission

MY REALITY CHECK **BOUNCED!**

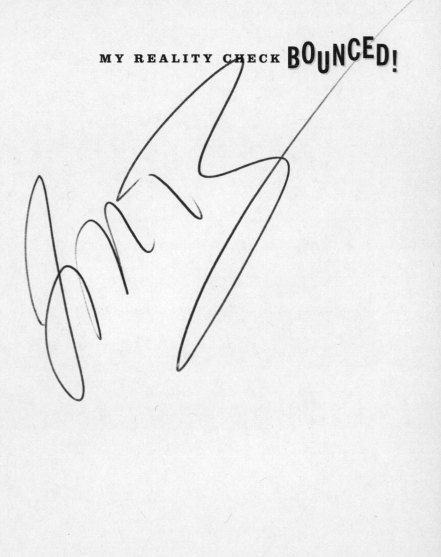

MY REALITY CHECK BOUNCED!

The Twentysomething's
Guide to Cashing In On
Your Real-World Dreams

JASON RYAN DORSEY

BROADWAY BOOKS

NEW YORK

PUBLISHED BY BROADWAY BOOKS

Copyright © 2007 by Jason Ryan Dorsey

Published in the United States by Broadway Books, an imprint
of The Doubleday Broadway Publishing Group, a division of
Random House, Inc., New York.
www.broadwaybooks.com

BROADWAY BOOKS and its logo, a letter B bisected on the
diagonal, are trademarks of Random House, Inc.

This title may be purchased for business or promotional use or
for special sales. For information, please write to: Special Markets
Department, Random House, Inc., 1745 Broadway, MD 6-3,
New York, NY 10019 or specialmarkets@randomhouse.com.

LIBRARY OF CONGRESS CATALOGING-IN-PUBLICATION DATA
Dorsey, Jason R. (Jason Ryan)
    My reality check bounced! : the twentysomething's guide to cashing
in on your real-world dreams / by Jason Ryan Dorsey. — 1st ed.
        p. cm.
    ISBN-13: 978-0-7679-2183-1 (alk. paper) 1. Success.
2. Self-actualization (Psychology) I. Title.

    BF637.S8D625 2007
    158.084'2—dc22

                                            2006012146

ISBN-13: 978-0-7679-2183-1
ISBN-10: 0-7679-2183-6

PRINTED IN THE UNITED STATES OF AMERICA

10 9 8 7 6 5 4 3 2 1

FIRST EDITION

*This book is dedicated to the
courageous twentysomethings
who bravely leave the paved path
to pursue their authentic path.*

CONTENTS

MY REALITY CHECK **BOUNCED!**

1

STAND UP FOR YOUR LIFE!

> We are all born unable to take care
> of ourselves. Living with meaning
> and purpose is a *learned* behavior.

REALITY-CHECK MOMENT—
THIS ISN'T WHAT I SIGNED UP FOR!

Tiffany, twenty-four, arrived distracted and anxious at the tiny coffee shop where we had agreed to meet. Despite her stylish business suit and expensive haircut and makeup, Tiffany had *the look*. I have seen it so often among twentysomethings in her situation. She was frustrated and disillusioned, wondering why her life just didn't feel right.

Tiffany thought she'd done everything she was supposed to. She made dean's list at her college and, after graduating, landed a great job. Now she was supposed to be spreading her wings, dating her true love, enjoying her career, and going on exciting adventures. Instead, the long hours and short tempers made her feel constantly on edge and insecure. She was asking herself the question about her place in life that haunts so many talented people in our generation: *"Is this it?"*

She felt trapped, stuck and confused. That's why she called me. She heard from a mutual friend that I helped people like her find their way again.

Tiffany ordered a double latte, then she cautiously confessed: She wasn't getting enough sleep. She didn't have time for her friends, family, or love life. She'd stopped working out. She was smoking too much. She wanted more freedom and sense of purpose. Despite working in a busy office six and sometimes seven days a week, she felt alone and lost. At twenty-four years old, Tiffany felt she was running hard *but going nowhere.*

"I never imagined I'd be in this position," she told me. "Maybe I was just young and naive, but I thought everything would fall into place and I'd love my life. It hasn't and I'm not. I'm stressed out all the time. I don't want to go to work; some days I don't even want to get out of bed. It's depressing. And I don't know what to do about it. I feel so confused. Nothing in college prepared me for this. Now I keep asking myself, *Is this what I worked so hard for?*"

Tiffany's reality check had bounced.

WELCOME TO THE REAL WHIRLED

Tiffany's not the only twentysomething who hasn't cashed in on her real-world dreams. Are you no longer a kid, but still unsure where you're headed or what your life's all about? Do you constantly find yourself settling for the safe path, rather than chasing what you most want? Are you spending hours downloading music or surfing the Web, chatting with friends on your cell phone, or watching late-night cable TV rather than living in the moment?

Are you helplessly watching your credit-card debt get bigger and bigger, while your relationships get shorter and shorter? Are you a victim of a bad economy, a mountain of college loans, or an egotistical boss? Are you living back in the house in which you grew up, sleeping in your old bedroom, pleading for gas money? Or do you find yourself trying to share one bathroom with five roommates? Do you still not have the love life you want, the friendships you want, the adventures you want, the home you want, the body you want, the career you want, the respect you want, and the clear sense of purpose you want?

To make matters more frustrating, you know you deserve better. You're smart. You can work hard when it matters. You know how to push yourself when you need to. You also were raised to think this was supposed to be one of the best times of your life, but it doesn't seem all that euphoric right now.

All these factors make your situation only more frustrating and, in some cases, depressing. Friends can see it on your face no matter how you try to hide it. They can hear it in your voice. You sense it as soon as you wake up in the morning. Your annoyance with your situation shows through in everything you do. You, too, might even have *the look*.

I know because I went through this soul-searching turmoil myself. And it's becoming an anthem for twentysomethings around the world. I hear it from recent college grads to twenty-nine-year-old corporate executives: How can doing everything right end up feeling wrong?

While you might long for a sense of purpose, direction, love, or belonging, someone else your age salivates over a 7 Series BMW or a job in New York City; but one thing you share with all twentysomethings is a determination to create success *on your own terms*.

That's what differentiates you from previous generations. You don't want to play by someone else's rules. You've seen what punching the clock nine to nine every day, sitting in an airless cubicle, playing the corporate schmooze game, and worshiping things at the expense of more meaningful dreams can do to a person's spirit, and you want no part of that. But what do you want?

Success on your own terms:
• To be free to enjoy sunny afternoons with friends, dance when no one is looking, and laugh out loud
• To be able to travel the world and learn about other cultures, ideas, and beliefs
• To pursue a clear and meaningful purpose
• To work with people you like, learn from, and respect
• To feel healthy, loved, and in love
• To make a difference in the world
• To use your talents, energy, and creativity
• To live in a place that feels like home
• To be respected
• To feel like your life means something

That's all part of filling the reality check void, and that's what this book is all about.

The challenge for you is that your vision of a meaningful, fulfilling life can conflict with an impersonal real world that does not want to accommodate your needs, ambition, personality, background, and perspective. It expects *you* to accommodate *it!* This creates an adversarial relationship that can make you feel powerless and grow into frustration, second guessing, confusion, and restlessness.

BREAKFAST WITH TIFFANY

Back at the coffee shop, I asked Tiffany what she could do to make her life more the way she wanted. I've found that most people who feel stuck like Tiffany know what they need to do.

They just haven't done it. Tiffany answered, "I need a job where I'm happy. That would be the biggest thing. I want to look forward to what I spend most of my day doing."

We talked about this for a while and came to the obvious conclusion that she needed either to somehow change her current work situation or to consider getting a different job. The only advice I gave her was something she had simply lost sight of in her frustration: *She was still in control of her life—* not her boss, best friend, roommates, or mom. Her life would start getting better *the moment* she stood up for herself.

Three weeks later, Tiffany and I met again at the tiny coffee shop. I was half expecting her to share some excuses as to why she hadn't done anything. Instead, *the look* was gone.

Tiffany was so excited to tell me what happened since our last conversation that I had to get her to slow down so I could get the story straight: Tiffany had decided that she was sick and tired of being overworked and underappreciated, so she told her boss exactly what was on her mind. At first he was flustered and insulted. Then he blamed her for the situation. "At the end of the week I was ready to quit," she said. "When suddenly my boss walks into my office, apologizes, and gives me a twenty-four-thousand-dollar raise and control of my schedule!"

We high-fived in the middle of the coffee shop!

Tiffany sipped her latte and then said, "I never saw how much control I had over my life until I used it. For a while there I really thought being unhappy was part of growing up and becoming an adult. I was scared. I was afraid that telling my boss how I felt might get me fired or make me look childish. I don't feel that way anymore. In fact, I think my frustration was an alarm telling me it was time to be honest with myself and start doing what was best for me."

Tiffany was beginning to see something that many twenty-somethings overlook as they are pushed around in the real world: You choose your own path. You choose where you work. You choose whom you date. You choose where you live. You choose what you study. You choose what you do in your free time. You choose, and those choices strung together become your life.

One year later Tiffany did leave her job. She took a new position in a coastal town. Now she likes where she works and the people she works with, she has a serious boyfriend with talk of marriage on the horizon, and she hangs out at the beach on the weekends. What a life! And she made it all happen by courageously standing up for her life and herself.

Tiffany, like you, had the power all along to start creating a life that felt meaningful and right. The only person who doubted that was herself. Not anymore.

> **BOUNCED:** My happiness is out of my hands.
> **CASHED:** How I feel about my life is determined by how I choose to live my life.

LET'S GET READY TO RUMBLE

You may think you found this book at just the right time. I think you're right! This book's message—to stand up and create the life you want—is precisely what you need to hear *now*. Part of your life, maybe the entire last few years, has left you wanting more meaning, inspiration, adventure, and purpose. It's time you do something about it. By picking this book as your guide, you are also telling the world that you want to pave this path on your own terms.

What you need are not excuses, money-back guarantees, or group hugs but time-tested strategies to get you on a better course. You usually pick up these strategies after years of being promoted through the school of hard knocks. But you don't want to wade through years of setbacks and sucker punches to learn how to feel alive. You want to use every resource and talent you can to get what you most want out of your life right *now*. Me, too!

Together we can.

Whether your vision for an awe-inspiring, meaningful life begins with

- Marrying your best friend
- Finding your life purpose
- Earning a promotion
- Starting your own business
- Graduating with a fancy degree
- Losing weight
- Climbing a mountain
- Changing the world

or something more intimate—*you have an idea of what you want your life to look, feel, taste, smell, and sound like.* At this precise moment, all that separates you from living that amazing experience are learning, action, and time.

Fortunately,

1. **You have chosen to learn.** This book will reveal what you need to know, some things you already know, and a few things you will never forget.

2. **You control your actions.** You determine when you apply what you know, so you can start benefiting from your smarts as soon as you are ready.

3. **Your future starts today!** The sooner you work to create the life you desire, the sooner you will have it!

YOU'VE GOT THE POWER

At twenty-four, Tiffany had to start living like she meant it if she was going to feel truly alive. No other person understood her hopes, dreams, memories, and fears the way she did. No other person understands *your* hopes, dreams, memories, and fears the way *you* do. Tiffany felt as if she were being smothered by her job and forced to silence her dreams. But settling for safe was *her choice*. All along Tiffany had the power to make her life the way she wanted it, and now she's doing just that. *Will you?*

You have ambitions and abilities; it's time they produced results. You have good ideas bouncing around in your head; it's time they came to life. You know in your heart you were born to do more, be more, and experience more. But only you can make what you believe to be possible spring to life. *Only you.*

If I've learned anything listening to and documenting so many different individual life stories, it's that finding your place in the world doesn't hinge on the impersonal real world. It hinges on *your world*. Once you let go of common twenty-something beliefs—such as "it's out of my control" and "it's not my fault" and "it's not the right time"—you will be free to start doing what it takes to get where you want. You will rise above your confusion and be able to live life on terms you establish and to get what you demand.

NO TIME LIKE THE PRESENT

Like Tiffany, you may have lost sight of your power to choose and, as a result, talked yourself out of control and into an unsatisfying rut. This is a challenging predicament and can be solved only by recognizing there will never be a magical right time to stand up for yourself and your future. All you have is right now. Until you see right now as the time to make changes for the better, you will continue feeling overwhelmed by your surroundings and situation. You will turn this feeling into excuses that keep you from breaking free such as: rent, car payments, credit-card bills, how your boss is unfair, how you need another degree, what your mom wants you to do . . . all of which only reinforce your unsatisfying holding pattern.

Waiting for any other time, especially the right time, to make your break for your dreams just wastes irreplaceable opportunities. You end up sitting on your dreams while your fears and insecurities take the lead. You continue getting older and more frustrated but not an inch closer to what will bring more meaning and satisfaction to your life, yet it's entirely your choice—even if you decide to ignore the fact that you choose the life you lead.

This was Tiffany's challenge. The more she stalled waiting for her situation to get better, the more helpless she felt. Unfortunately, most twentysomethings never experience a neon-bright moment of divine intervention or profound clarity that inspires them to finally leap after their dreams. Instead, with each passing year of not being satisfied and not doing anything about it, they grow more reluctant to take the risks necessary to create the outcomes they long for. Before they know it, they look back and wonder where all that time went. *You deserve better.*

You deserve to be excited about each and every day. You deserve to wake up feeling confident, inspired, and on the right track. You deserve to go to sleep beside your best friend secure in the fact your life means something. You deserve to give yourself a chance to make this happen.

GETTING A GRIP

Your true passion for life will surface only when you take responsibility for creating the life you want. Until you do this, other people and events will choose for you. And your boss, neighbor, parents, and old high-school friends don't have nearly as much riding on your happiness and fulfillment as you do. Taking responsibility for your future gives you the choice to put everything you have into getting what you want, whether that is inner peace or a purple Porsche.

Tiffany, like you, was standing at a real-world crossroad. She was going to either let her reality check keep bouncing or cash in on her courage. She made the right choice and so can you.

HOW DO I KNOW ALL THIS?

Because I've been there, done that. I've dedicated the last nine years of my life to listening to and helping people who feel frustrated, beaten down, uninspired, trapped, and lost. To accomplish this I've traveled over a million miles and talked with more than five hundred thousand people about what makes life worth living.

My quest has taken me from quiet ranches in Kansas to bustling ports in Maine to crowded cities in Egypt, Finland, and Spain. I've been hired to advise some of the wealthiest twentysomethings in the world. I've freely helped thousands more scratching by in abject poverty. I've built a thriving career teaching ordinary people how to break free and live extraordinary lives.

In the process, I've learned all of us have room to grow. Rich kids in the suburbs taught me that we all have insecurities we must address. Children I've met who survived genocide taught me that there is no limit to human resilience. Twentysomethings who graduated from Ivy League colleges and then moved in with their moms showed me that *potential alone does not guarantee success*. Most of all, I've learned that making your life the way you want it starts with jumping in with both feet.

At eighteen years old, I risked everything I had to follow my gut by leaving college as a junior to write a book. This was the scariest—and in my parents' view at the time dumbest—decision I've ever made. I had worked hard to start college earlier than normal and had great job offers awaiting my graduation. By withdrawing from school I was trading my path to Wall Street riches for the unknown hardships of living with meaning. I had no idea what I was getting into, *only what I was leaving behind*.

I left college because I felt the path that I was on—the standard go to college, get a good job, get married, make babies, and so on—was no longer inspiring. The one passion I had was helping people who, like me, came from challenging backgrounds. I thought writing a practical book teaching young people how to get a head start on the real world could make a difference.

I wrote that book in my college dorm room at age eighteen. Writing the book took me three weeks—it's amazing how fast you can type when your future is riding on it. Then I borrowed money from everyone I knew and paid to publish the book myself. This was the only way I could think to get the book in to the hands of the young people who I thought could most benefit from it.

Having spent all my borrowed money on publishing the book, I wound up spending the next year sleeping on the floor of a friend's garage apartment. Every day I went around my city telling anyone who would listen what I was up to. That

entire year I lived on about $4 per day (I can cook ramen noo-
dles *thirty-eight ways*). Before turning nineteen, I managed to
ring up over $50,000 in debt thanks to loans, credit cards, and
business lines of credit. My friends were impressed, and my
parents were terrified.

Progress that first year was excruciatingly slow. Sometimes
I felt as if I were going in circles, and other times I felt as if I
were repeatedly hitting my head on a concrete wall. So many
nights I went to sleep on the cheap beige carpet depressed and
frustrated. My big break came when I was invited to speak to
a group of students and teachers about my book. In this one
speech to forty people, my message found an audience. They
told other people who told other people, which led to more
speeches and more books.

Over 1,550 schools and colleges eventually adopted my first
book, *Graduate to Your Perfect Job*, as required reading. That
launched me into keynoting conferences for everyone from
corporate executives and wealthy entrepreneurs to community events for gang leaders, college students, and single parents. In three years, I went from sleeping on a garage floor to
meeting the president of the United States and sharing what I
had learned on national television shows such as the *Today*
show and *The View*.

A DISTURBING TREND

All that led back to more conversations with people my age
about what weighed most heavily on their minds.

In the last few years, those conversations took on a consistently disturbing tone. Smart people in their twenties from all
walks of life were calling and e-mailing me with their frustration and discontent. They felt unexpectedly uninspired about
their place in the world.

Their angst ran deeper than money, titles, and degrees. They were expecting the real world to bring them *happiness, meaning,* and *purpose;* but instead it brought confusion and second guessing.

This crisis hit close to home. I had been through this turmoil, and it led me to leave college and write my first book. That one big leap of faith put me on a course that has been inspiring and rewarding. But many of my friends and contacts were not feeling so lucky or confident. From the outside they looked okay, but inside they were slowly falling apart.

They dealt with their growing dissatisfaction in a number of ways: one-night stands, maxing out their credit cards, weekend drinking binges, moving in with Mom, changing jobs frequently, and questioning their previous decisions. Underneath it all, they felt unsettled and alone. I heard this story so many times, I felt I had to do something to help. I became intensely focused on addressing this twentysomething search for meaning.

HOW THIS BOOK WORKS

Each chapter of this book is packed with stories of real twentysomethings—plus a few older and a few younger—who have survived the ups and downs of life just like you and me. These are everyday people who have chosen to look deep inside their heart, mind, and soul to figure out who they are and where they are going. This questioning allowed them to have earth-shaking epiphanies that changed their life; the same thing can happen to you.

Walking a few miles in their shoes will stretch you in new directions, because they've dared to not settle, defied defeat, and broke free from the prison of indecision and insecurity. Looking at the world through their eyes, you can reap their gain without their pain. These stories will also serve as a reminder that you're not alone but one part of a larger movement toward meaning, which is taking place around the globe.

Weaving the stories together are *specific actions* you can immediately use to escape from your restlessness. These actions will get you unstuck, on fire, and back in control. That's why it's necessary for you complete the interactive sections in the book *as you read*. (Yes, write in this book! Forget what your sixth-grade English teacher said, you bought this book so you have the right to write in it and make it your own!) The interactive sections are brief and a bit challenging, but the payoffs to you will be huge.

As a bonus, if you're *really ready* to start getting more out of your life, I've included a few "Reality Check Challenges." These challenges will push you to go to some places you may not want to go. But once you do, your perception, confidence, and direction will be transformed.

As Tiffany learned, feeling inspired about your life comes from taking responsibility for creating the life you want. This book contains the practical, real-world knowledge you've been looking for *to get from where you are now to where you want to be*. In your hands are the steps you need to take to make your life as fulfilling as you want. But only you can make it happen. Once you finish reading, you have a choice: either put it off until tomorrow or live like you mean it today. I vote you live it. Time will be on your side once you start making the most of what you have *now*.

INSTANT MESSAGE

▶ You never realize how much control you have until you use it!

▶ Right now is the right time to start living like you mean it.

▶ Time is on your side once you act like today matters.

BOUNCED: My happiness is out of my hands.

CASHED: How I feel about my life is determined by how I choose to live my life.

ONLINE: Find out where Tiffany is now at **www.myrealitycheckbounced.com/book**

2

BREAK FREE

> To see into the future all you have to
> do is *close* your eyes.

REALITY-CHECK MOMENT—
I'M STILL LIVING AT MY PARENTS' HOUSE!

Do you know any "boomerangers"? People your age who
thought they knew what they wanted, moved away from home
for work or school or a relationship, only to retreat a few
months or years later to their childhood bedroom, living off
their parents and feeling as if they've failed?

Join the club.

Again and again, I meet people who are so excited to get
out of high school, college, or graduate school and start life
with a bang, only to be greeted instead with a buzzkill. After
trying their hand in the real world they're frustrated, confused, and barely getting by. They dreamed they'd be free and
independent, but now they're negotiating curfews with Dad
and car insurance with Mom. Even if they have managed to
live on their own—if that's what you call living with *twelve*
roommates—they're finding less fulfillment than they
thought. Many of them lie awake at night wondering if they
actually have what it takes to ever make it on their own. This
is not the launch into adulthood they dreamed about.

Josh, twenty-seven, is a boomeranger who was able to break free of this frustrating spiral and never look back. In two years, he went from a confused college graduate crashing at his mom's in Dallas to a rising corporate star living in his very own house in Atlanta. I was so curious about how he found his way that I bought him dinner to hear his story:

As a kid, I always thought I'd grow up to be a doctor like my parents. I took the premed path in college, but ultimately decided that wasn't the career for me.

With no obvious career path, college graduation approaching, and my apartment lease ending, I made the safe choice and moved back home with my mom in Dallas. It was awkward sleeping in my old bedroom, but I felt like I had nowhere else to go.

One evening I was watching TV at home and noticed some old family photos on the wall. Looking at those pictures, I saw a big truth staring back at me. I was essentially in the same place where I had started four years before. This realization made me very uncomfortable, especially since I had always imagined myself climbing some prestigious corporate ladder. I never could have predicted I'd be living back home with my mom after college.

Both my parents immigrated to the United States from India in the late sixties for a chance to live the American dream. They started with nothing and worked hard to build successful careers. Their hard work paid off and afforded me the luxury to go to prep school, travel overseas, and attend an expensive liberal arts college. And what had I done with all their generosity and unwavering support? I was still eating my mom's food, living under her roof, and depending on her to pay for gas in my car.

Looking at those old family photos I decided I'd spent too much time and effort to give up so easily and settle back where

I started. I knew I had to somehow find out what I was supposed to do with my life. The only way to do this would be to step out of my comfortable "Mom safety net." That would force me to stop hiding from the real world and start figuring out whatever I was supposed to do with my life. I had to leave my mom's house, leave Dallas, leave my old friends, and move some place where I had no one to fall back on except myself.

My flash of courage was offset by one big hesitation. To make this jump, I'd have to find a new job in a new city where I knew no one. And I'd have to learn how to be okay on my own. From the warmth of my mom's house, those were pretty chilling obstacles. But I just couldn't see myself mooching off my mom another day—she'd already paid so much for my education and I felt guilty not using it.

By this time, I had already landed an entry-level job at a stock brokerage, so I showed up for work the next morning and told my boss I was moving to Atlanta. He didn't grasp how starting over in another city would help me find my way in the world, but he did offer to call our Atlanta office and put in a good word for me. I had worked for my boss for two months, so his sticking his neck out for my future was totally unexpected. That taught me my first big lesson about making it in the real world: If you're brave enough to share your ambitions, people may just be brave enough to help.

From my boss's one phone call, I lined up three job interviews in Atlanta the very next week. I bought my first U.S. map, packed some dress clothes, and drove the twelve highway hours to get there.

The interviews went okay. I was nervous and assumed my jitters undermined my strengths. I wasn't aware enough to know that driving to another state for a job interview took guts. Apparently this was what the interviewers wanted. They made me a job offer before I could get back to Dallas! I know this sounds too good or easy to be true, but I had never taken such a big risk with my future, so I didn't know what to expect.

Back in Dallas I packed only what would fit in my car and drove straight to Atlanta. My friends kept calling my cell with their reasons why I shouldn't move. They told me how tough it was going to be starting over in a new city with no friends or family nearby. But the more my friends tested my resolve, the more I understood why my move to Atlanta scared them. They were in the same place I had been one week before, watching life pass by from the safety of their parents' couch. By getting off my mom's couch and starting from scratch in a new city, I challenged their laziness. If I made it in Atlanta, even in a small way, they might have to take a new look at their dependence. I listened to their concerns but kept driving. If they were right, I'd be home in six months anyway.

My first night in Atlanta, I thought they were right. I didn't know anyone, I had no furniture, I had no TV, I had no idea what I was getting into, and I couldn't sleep. Sitting on the floor of my empty apartment I just kept thinking, "What the hell am I doing here?"

THE BEST DECISION I EVER MADE

You get wise fast when you throw yourself into the world. Since moving to Atlanta three years ago, I've had to figure out for myself what makes me happy, what pushes me to work hard, what makes me get up early and stay out late. I've learned how to deal with failure, uncertainty, skeptics, and difficult people. I've learned to trust myself and be open to acting on whatever life has to offer.

I wanted to run a marathon, so I did it. I wanted to meet new people, so I took a second job at night at a restaurant. I wanted to move up in my firm, so I became one of the youngest people ever promoted to my position. I wanted to have my own place, so I saved and bought a house. Sure, my life in Atlanta hasn't always been easy or fun, but it has stretched me to look inside for what I was missing. I'm not sure that would've ever happened if I were still living with my mom in Dallas.

You never look at your world the same way once you start making it on your own. Now I'm not afraid to go after what I really want. I'm not afraid to make new friends, ask for help, or take a risk that other people think is a bit crazy. Moving to Atlanta has taught me that when I put my life in my own hands, I have the power to make it work. I think not knowing what I was capable of doing was a big part of the uncertainty I felt about where I should go with my life. Moving to Atlanta changed all that.

WHERE ARE *YOU* GOING?

Josh's story might sound familiar if you've been feeling unsure of your abilities or where to go next. But once you do decide where you want to go with your life, you can put *everything you have* into making that vision real.

Right now you probably have some idea of the life you'd like to have or at least some clue as to where you want to be next year and the year after that. Maybe this image is crystal clear to you and has been since you were ten years old. Maybe you're just starting to think past next weekend. Whatever your situation, the more you see yourself with a specific, meaningful future, the more motivation and courage you will have to live it.

Why? Because when you know where you want to go, and why, *you can identify and then take the actions necessary to get there.* Painting a clear picture of the future you want is a critical step in breaking free of your restlessness because it tells you and the world that you have a future,—and the power to create it! You also make it much easier to find a path toward that future when you know where you are going.

Think about it: How do you stop spinning your wheels if you don't know where you're going? How do you know if you've reached your goals if you don't know what your goals look and feel like? How do you get the right people to help you if you can't tell them the kind of help you need? You can answer all these questions *and* free yourself to do what you've always wanted by creating and then locking on to a personally meaningful picture of the future you demand to live. This picture of where you want to go should be so motivating that you will push yourself to do whatever it takes to see it through.

Okay, okay, I can just hear you saying, "But I *don't* know where I see myself in the future." Or "I feel stuck because I *don't* know what will make me happy." Or "There are just too many choices and what if I make the wrong one: Should I get a real job now or backpack across Europe? Should I settle down in a serious relationship or play the field? Should I move back home until I figure this out or share a one-bedroom apartment with four roommates? Do I have to go in a direction that is already well traveled or can I make a new path that better fits who I am?"

To begin solving the riddle of where to go with your life, you must be willing to look inside for the answers. You must be honest about what inspires, delights, and excites you. When you look inside yourself, you will see that you have all the ingredients for creating a picture of your ideal adult life. My goal is to help you construct this picture and make it so vivid that it becomes your life. Once you have this mental picture, you will be able to make tough decisions faster, learn lessons you didn't see before, and brave the risks inherent in any new venture. This picture will burn so strong inside you that you will see it through, even if the entire world seems to be against you.

You will persist because you have within yourself a clear reason to live.

GET YOUR FUTURE IN FOCUS

I call this tantalizing image of where you want to be and what you want to experience your Future Picture. It's an emotional, mental, physical, and spiritual molding of what your life would be like *if you could wave a magic wand and make it just the way you want it.* You've already seen in Chapter 1 what taking responsibility for your future can do for freeing your spirit and independence. Creating this Future Picture funnels all your talent, creativity, resilience, and energy down one meaningful path so you can put everything you've got into getting where you most want to be.

Davis, twenty-eight, has experienced the personal reward that comes from focusing all his efforts toward one clear vision. When he was in college, he dreamed about opening his own movie theater. He saw his movie theater as an entire entertainment experience. He imagined serving food like they do at regular restaurants, offering adult beverages of every flavor, and showcasing movies that were not just big-budget, mainstream productions. Davis saw this vision so clearly he could tell you how the seats were going to look, what the staff was going to wear, and what type of nostalgic posters would hang on the walls.

Opening a movie theater, especially with no experience, is a long shot at best. But Davis saw it in his mind, and he knew what he had to do. He worked long hours seven days a week to turn his vision into a reality. Four years after leaving college, Davis cut the red ribbon that officially opened his movie theater. The seats, uniforms, and posters looked exactly like he had imagined. So did the crowds. The movie theater he had seen in his mind for so long was such a hit that he's already opening a second one!

When you emotionally, intellectually, physically, and spiritually lock onto a vision of the future you want to create, you give yourself *no wiggle room* to hide behind excuses, insecurities, setbacks, and fears. With the right Future Picture to guide your way, you won't allow yourself only to talk about your dreams in your pajamas. That's because your Future Picture will be so mesmerizing that you won't settle for less. You'll make sure to live it because it will be exactly what you are looking for.

BOUNCED: I don't know what I want to do with my life.

CASHED: My Future Picture is so enticing, I'll do whatever it takes to live it.

DESTINY IS IN THE DETAILS

The details within your Future Picture are what help you commit to the life you know is possible. Details require you to think through the entire experience and concentrate on the decisions you will face. All this makes the future you want feel more within your reach. As you become familiar with the smallest details in your Future Picture, you will begin to spot those same details in your daily endeavors. They will serve as reminders of the path you are on and the destination you have chosen.

With a fully detailed Future Picture you will be able to stretch yourself with confidence toward new limits and get the most out of each adventure. Having a powerful picture of the future may seem like common sense, yet most twentysomethings, especially those feeling uninspired in the real world, have lost touch with what most brings meaning to their life. That's a big part of why they feel stuck and unfulfilled—they don't know where to go to find what they are missing. Answer for yourself: Where will you have your fortieth birthday party? Who will be there? What will you look like? Who will give you your first birthday kiss? What will be your favorite birthday gift?

For those of you who are still feeling unsure or skeptical about constructing a highly detailed Future Picture, I've found the following questions can reveal helpful clues.

ABOUT YOUR IDEAL CAREER

1. What shoes will you wear to work?
2. What will your workplace sound like at 3:00 P.M.
3. What will be your main responsibility?
4. Who will you talk most with on the phone?
5. What will you get paid annually?

ABOUT YOUR IDEAL FAMILY LIFE

1. What photos will hang in your living room?
2. What will you do with your family on Saturdays?
3. What will be the view from your front door?
4. What family tradition will you start?
5. What will your grandkids brag about you the most?

ABOUT YOUR IDEAL PERSONAL LIFE

1. How will you physically feel when you wake up?
2. How will you relax each day?
3. What book will be on your bedside?
4. What do you spend the most time doing outside of work?
5. What makes you feel most alive?

ABOUT WHAT YOUR LIFE MEANS

1. What will your friends and family say to strangers about you?
2. What is the greatest memory you will have?
3. How will you help people without showing up?
4. What will be your biggest legacy to the world?
5. What will people say at your funeral?

Some of these questions may seem straight out of left field, but each one challenges you to take another glimpse into who you are and where you want to go. The better you know yourself and your desires, the easier it is to turn them into a life of meaning. By answering these questions, you have begun to declare to yourself and the world that you are ready to live your life to its fullest!

TIME TO TAKE YOUR FUTURE PICTURE

Now that you've answered the questions about your ideal life, you are primed to begin crafting your personalized Future Picture. Of course, this vision for your future may change as you do, but you have to start somewhere. Remember, when it comes to your Future Picture, destiny is in the details. The more emotional, inspiring, and meaningful the picture you create, the more you will buy into it so strongly that you will do whatever it takes to make it real. This picture then becomes the future you choose, the future you seek, and the future you live.

Your Future Picture is a combination of four snapshots that represent one primary piece of your quest for meaning.

Your Career Snapshot

Your career snapshot includes all aspects of your professional career from the education you need, the position you aspire to hold, the people you want on your team, the financial security you desire, the major achievements you want to accomplish, and what you want your career to signify. By this point in your life, you probably have had a few jobs and tried on a few different career paths. Reflecting on these past experiences may be particularly helpful in designing an inspiring career snapshot.

Your Family Snapshot

A family snapshot includes all aspects of family, from the one that raised you to the one you want to raise. Make sure to fill in every detail: Would you like to get married? Have kids? Where will you take family vacations? How will you raise your kids? Where will your family live? Who will attend family reunions? As a twentysomething, you've had your share of family ups and downs. These should give you extra insight into what you want in the people you plan to share your life with.

Your Personal Snapshot

Your mental and physical well being is your personal snapshot. Pay special attention to how you want your body to look and feel. Then focus on how you will spend your free time, how you will challenge yourself to keep growing, what kind of friends you will have, and all the hobbies and interests that will add spice to your life. If you can't think of any engaging hobbies or personal interests, concentrate instead on the kind of person you intend to be and what you want to pursue outside of work and family.

Your Purpose Snapshot

The purpose snapshot is all about the bigger, deeper, more intimate goals of your life. For you this might be a religious calling, a spiritual journey, or another path to meaning that makes your heart feel peace and contentment. Your purpose snapshot should be an intangible thread that runs through all your other snapshots. Understanding, defining, and living this purpose is a lifelong quest, and it benefits you to understand and undertake it as early in life as possible.

After writing and refining each of these four snapshots individually, imagine each one as a piece of a larger puzzle. Separately they don't hold all the fulfillment, answers, or meaning you desire; but when brought together, they are what your life would be like if you lived it to its fullest.

With a detailed, well-thought-out picture of your future, you have taken one of the biggest insurance policies you can to keep from ever feeling stuck, lost, helpless, or trapped. Your Future Picture can and will change as you gain the perspective that comes with age, but just knowing that you are heading somewhere valuable can be a freeing revelation. Your Future Picture also allows you to see how the present connects with the future so you can make the most of today and tomorrow.

Take a few moments to summarize each of your four snapshots in one or two sentences, so you have them for easy reference. For example, for your career snapshot, you might write down something like this: "Owning my own interior design company." For your purpose snapshot you might write: "Living each day with meaning while helping others do the same."

Your career snapshot:

_____

Your family snapshot:

_____

Your personal snapshot:

_____

Your purpose snapshot:

_____

If you are really ready to see these four snapshots come to life, then write them on the mirror in your bathroom, in the cover of the journal or notepad you keep by your bed, and on a piece of paper you carry in your purse or wallet. Whenever you are feeling challenged, discouraged, or frustrated, read these sentences until the images come to life in your imagination. Then you will put yourself in the right frame of mind to tackle whatever has distressed you.

FYI: It's okay if you don't have a clear vision for one or more of your snapshots. The simple act of opening yourself to the idea that your future is not some spooky thing out of your control but an experience that you create is a powerful step forward.

With the picture you have for your future, take a moment to notice the following:

1. **Which of your four snapshots was easiest to describe?**

_____

- This shows the area of your journey that so far is or has been your top priority. The more effort you put into thinking about or doing something the more real it becomes to you. This is why if you've been focused on your career you probably have a pretty clear picture of where you want that to go. The same holds true if you are ready for a serious relationship. You know what you want, and you keep a lookout for it. The easier it is for you to describe your ideal future in one area of your four snapshots, the more confidence you have in your abilities to make it happen.

2. Which of your four snapshots was most difficult to describe?

---

* This reveals the area of your life where you have the most insecurity or have unintentionally chosen not to venture. Maybe you are unclear about this part of your life because it has not been a priority, because you have tried a few things and none has fit, or for some reason it makes you uncomfortable to go there. Recognize that you have room to grow in this area, and at some point you will need to address it to live with the meaning you desire.

I've watched thousands of people get a better grip on who they are and where they are going after describing these four snapshots. In the countless snapshots I've read, I have yet to read two that are exactly the same. That reinforces to me how a purposeful life is your own personal journey and not some mass-marketed self-help informercial destination. What fires you up to take a huge leap of faith in yourself may seem like a waste of time and energy to somebody else. This doesn't mean that one of you is right and the other wrong, just that you have your own view of the world and that's what you need to stay true to. Your parents, friends, and society as a whole have a vision of success that they will try to impress on you, but that may not match who you are. If you give in and pursue a path to appease someone else, *anyone else*, you can end up with big regrets or the hollow satisfaction that comes from meaningless success. Be true to your authentic Future Picture and the future you create will be authentically fulfilling.

BABY STEPS LEAD TO BREAKTHROUGHS

If you're still hesitant or skeptical about the idea of a Future Picture, don't stress. Just recognize that your future is an outgrowth of your actions and choices taken *today*. Every decision you make, every person you meet, every opportunity you explore either moves you further away or closer to the future you desire. Knowing this, you can make the choices and take the actions that get you on a path to what you most want for yourself.

If you are at a crossroad of indecision and are uncertain about where to turn, look inside yourself and you will find the answer by asking the right questions. Here's a few: Do you feel most inspired when you are helping other people? What actions and interactions add the most significance to your day? Do you feel most alive when you go to the beach, the office, or venture off on your own? Does you heart beat faster when you are passed by an exotic car or when you slow down to check out a new exhibit at your local museum? Do you think you are more happy constantly being on the move or staying in one place for a while? What actions and direction make you most enjoy a regular Wednesday in March?

If you're one of the people who prefer to talk about what's wrong in your life rather than what's right or feels good, you may have to rely on what you *don't* like to reveal what you *do* like. This approach is just like going to a restaurant and knowing beforehand that you don't like fish. You can skip all the fish items and focus only on the options that are left. Maybe you've proved to yourself that you're not happy working with other people or being in high-pressure environments or interacting with babies. Maybe you don't like working outdoors, being paid on commission, or traveling overseas. Getting clear on what you don't want for your future can provide helpful hints to getting on the path that best matches your desires.

Once you have a Future Picture—perfectly clear or a work in progress—you are ready to take the actions that will provide the confidence, insight, and experiences you need to get there. With each step you take toward your Future Picture, your next step will become clearer. Take enough steps forward, and you put your reality check back in check.

Here are some inspiring real-life examples.

Twenty-three-year-old Carrie always thought she wanted to be a TV reporter. She worked hard and landed an internship at a small news station. Soon it became clear that being a TV reporter wasn't right for her. At first, she was bummed out, but then she tried some other positions at the news station and realized she loved directing. Now she's changed her major and is working her contacts to land a position as an assistant to a director upon graduation.

Tanya, twenty-nine, always thought she wanted a man with a wild streak who liked to be spontaneous and challenge authority. She dated lots of these guys and then realized that, while they were fun for a short time, the sparkle always wore off. So she took a chance and started dating a highly disciplined guy in the army. He was basically the exact opposite of all her previous relationships. They were married six months later.

Arnold, twenty-eight, had been overweight since he returned to grad school. He just couldn't muster the strength to get in shape with so much school work to be done. After his graduation, he was complaining about his weight, so his wife suggested he stop making excuses and join a running club. He had never been much of a runner and was worried that the other people might laugh at him or, worse, leave him behind.

He finally gave in and went on one run with a local running club. Eighteen months later he had lost thirty pounds and completed his first half marathon!

Joe was raised in a strict, conservative religious family, but he never felt complete with his spiritual connection. At twenty-four, he decided that there had to be something out there for him, so he cashed in his savings and flew to India with only a picture of the place he wanted to visit. He credits that one adventure, more than going to college or grad school or moving out on his own or having his first real job, as the most personally defining experience of his twenties.

DREAM IT. TEST IT. BELIEVE IT. LIVE IT.

The bigger and bolder your Future Picture the more effort and creativity it will require for you to reach it. This may seem scary at first, but it will grow to become inspiring because the challenges to reaching your Future Picture are a big part of what makes living it so meaningful. Whether your Future Picture is bold or basic, you probably won't reach it tomorrow, this week, or even this year. But every day you reach for it you move closer to getting there. It's these daily, incremental baby steps that are critical to positioning you for life-changing breakthroughs.

However, I understand that you may not be overly thrilled to take lots of baby steps to get where you ultimately want to go. So as a twentysomething who appreciates the power of instant gratification, I've created Reality Check Challenge 1 to show you what's in store if you stay faithful to your dreams. Complete this challenge, and you can touch your future in the present.

REALITY CHECK CHALLENGE

GOAL: Sample with all your senses how rewarding your Future Picture will feel.

TASK: If your vision for your future hinges on financial freedom, I challenge you to test-drive the most expensive car you can or to tour a mega-million-dollar mansion that is for sale. If your Future Picture consists of you having a loving and happy family, I challenge you to volunteer at a local elementary school or nursing home. If your Future Picture requires you advancing your formal education, I challenge you to sit in on a class at the most prestigious university in your area. If your Future Picture necessitates you finding your spiritual calling, I challenge you to attend three different religious or spiritual services and see what you like. Whatever your Future Picture, I challenge you to find a way to taste, touch, smell, hear, and see it *right now*. You don't need anyone's permission to try on your dreams—all you need is a little creativity!

Only a few of you are so committed to living your Future Picture that you will take on Reality Check Challenge 1. If you are one of those who will tour your dream home, manage a room full of lively kids, interview local business owners, or sit in on an unfamiliar religious service—you should be very proud of yourself. You have taken an important step toward proving to yourself how much control you have over your life and future.

If you were given a brochure after test-driving your dream car, pin it to a wall in your bedroom. If you received a thank-you note from the children or elderly persons you volunteered to help, keep it where you can read it if you begin to feel frustrated or underappreciated. If you sat in on a university class, make the university's home page a favorite in your Web browser. Keep these mementos of the future that you want within reach, so you always have something to remind you of where you are going.

As you move closer to the future you think you want, you will become more certain of the future you *really* want. As your confidence grows in the direction you have chosen, so will your enthusiasm for the path you are taking. Be open to what most feels right *to you*, and you will get to what is most right *for you*.

From the familiar confines of his mom's couch, Josh was able to see beyond his family photos and create a mental picture for his own future that was worth pursuing. This took him from feeling frustrated and confused to inspired and in control. Three years later, he lived the rewarding life he imagined. You will, too, once you harness the power of your own Future Picture.

INSTANT MESSAGE
- ▶ The future you want starts with a compelling mental picture.
- ▶ The more details you add to your Future Picture, the more you will believe you can make it happen.
- ▶ To bring your future to life try it on in the present.

BOUNCED: I don't know what I want to do with my life.

CASHED: My Future Picture is so enticing, I'll do whatever it takes to live it.

ONLINE: Hear Josh share more about making his big move to Atlanta at **www.myrealitycheckbounced.com/book**

3

LIGHT YOUR FIRE

> Dreams reveal possibilities. Passion
> determines whether you live them.

REALITY-CHECK MOMENT—
IS IT ALWAYS GOING TO BE THIS HARD TO GET OUT OF BED?

Many people I've talked to have problems coming up with
their Future Picture; or once they do, they doubt they've chosen the "right" one. So they procrastinate, avoiding the path
that would make them happy, or they get busy with a million
trivial things rather than focusing on fulfilling their dreams.
The longer these people choose to stay adrift the more helpless and empty they feel.

A few years ago, Ben found himself in this very predicament. He was seventeen and could not shake the depression
that held him hostage through high school. His girlfriend had
already attempted suicide. In deepening despair, he severed
relations with his family. That led him to move into the nasty
basement of a trashy bar in Manhattan. His new home had no
windows, no comforts of any kind, just a makeshift six by
eight room with a concrete floor converted from unused stor-
age space. Roaches fought for every square inch.

An older friend, Leslie, recognized Ben's downward spiral.
She knew he needed direction and encouragement. She found

him sitting alone in the basement and persuaded him to go for a walk. She said she had something important to show him.

She took Ben to the mammoth headquarters of the United Nations, where she often went on her own contemplative walks. Foreign accents echoed in the halls, while starched diplomats scurried to high-security offices. Ben felt intimidated walking around the cavernous building, but for some reason he did not want to leave.

Ben was awed watching so many diverse people working together to unite and improve the world. After living throughout Europe and the United States as a child, Ben understood why this international teamwork was so needed. He took all the free UN literature he could get his hands on, and asked Leslie lots of questions on the walk home.

Like delegates at the UN, Ben was concerned about the genocide extinguishing thousands of lives overseas. He was also concerned that young people his own age were dying in other countries because they didn't have clean drinking water. He was concerned that innocent kids as young as six and seven years old were being sold into slavery. But what could he do? He was cut off from his family and was sleeping in a room underneath a bar.

The energy and sense of purpose Ben felt walking inside the UN was something he had never experienced before. He found himself unable to sleep or even think about anything else. After a few days, his suicidal thoughts disappeared for good. Ben had replaced them with something much more potent: a vision for his future that suddenly gave his life meaning.

PASSION TO THE RESCUE

Uncovering this passion was Ben's big step out of depression, confusion, apathy, and self-doubt. He saw himself becoming a catalyst that would connect youth around the world with each other to solve local and global problems. Ben grabbed on to this crazy vision with two hands.

For three months after his impromptu tour of the UN, Ben researched the organization's history, accomplishments, and missteps. He examined hundreds of UN resolutions regarding young people. Then he carefully submitted to the UN his own proposal to spearhead the creation of a United Nations Youth Assembly.

The UN's reply was swift and direct: "Use our name again, and you will have to deal with our legal department." However, the boilerplate rejection only solidified Ben's resolve. He saw so much pain, anger, hate, and prejudice in the world. He knew youth had some of the answers. All that young people needed to put these answers into action was a way to come together and candidly express them.

Word of Ben's proposal made the rounds on the Internet. A man in Arizona was intrigued that such a young guy would make such a bold proposal. He contacted Ben and offered him free room and board if he promised to relentlessly pursue his vision of connecting young people around the world. Ben moved from the confines of his concrete basement to the Arizona desert, where he had the space and encouragement to think big—and to take action.

In 2000, after spending two years working full time on his vision without receiving a single paycheck, Ben moved back to New York City to launch his international youth network. In New York, he worked around the clock networking, partnering, protesting, fund-raising, and advocating. Ben's organization, the Global Youth Action Network (GYAN), was going from a picture in his mind to reality.

Ben's dedication, passion, and selflessness—he paid himself only enough to rent a space in a *different* basement—won him intense loyalty from grassroots youth leaders around the world. These leaders showed their support by linking Ben's organization to thousands of international youth organization, in only two years.

In 2002, Ben's efforts reached critical mass. The GYAN helped Youth Service America lead Global Youth Service Day. This initiative mobilized more than one million young people in 150 countries over the course of one weekend. All these young people came together on the same weekend to better themselves, their communities, and the future of the world.

In Afghanistan, youth held roundtables to share their vision for the country. In Togo, youth participated in AIDS walks for awareness and education. In Russia, over seventeen hundred service projects were led by youth. Across the globe, presidents and heads of state publicly talked about the importance of empowering youth in areas such as education, health care, employment, and voting.

Global Youth Service Day became one of the largest international youth-led initiatives *in history*. Ben's vast network of youth organizations was instrumental in the initiative's success. Just as Ben imagined at age eighteen standing spellbound in the halls of the UN building, youth could come together to better the world, if given the chance.

Since the UN first rejected his proposal, Ben has spoken there many times. His Global Youth Action Network is now an official partner of the UN system. Every day, he receives hundreds of emotional e-mails from youth in distant countries thanking him for his work and asking how they can get involved with GYAN.

Now twenty-seven, Ben still sleeps in a room in a basement apartment that he bricked himself. He has almost no savings. He has no retirement plan. He pays his staff when he cannot afford to pay himself. He never complains. He just presses on.

He views each day as a gift, because each day he gets to live his passion.

SO WHAT EXACTLY IS PASSION?

Passion is the simmering energy inside all of us that boils over when we are living our greatest, most authentic purpose. Passion is the natural buzz that keeps you working late into the night when others have called it quits. Passion is the commitment you feel in your stomach when you push yourself to your personal best.

What motivated Ben to help starving kids in foreign countries while he was living hand to mouth sleeping on a basement floor? What kept him going when the UN rejected his youth assembly proposal? What gave him the courage to move to the desert to follow his vision of a better world? What inspired him, a young guy with no college degree, few friends, and zero savings to put his crazy dream into action? PASSION!

Passion is *burning desire that drives dedicated action.* Ben desired, more than anything else in the world, to empower youth to come together to solve local and global problems. This passion permeated his every thought, action, dream, and breath. His spirit was on fire to help young people he would most likely never meet. Discovering this passion transformed him from a suicidal kid sleeping on a basement floor to working directly with world leaders as well as with disenfranchised young people who never before had a voice.

True to his character, Ben downplays his role. You won't ever see him on national TV asking for donations or dropping names about the leaders who call him for advice. However, the countless lives GYAN has affected say more than he ever could.

Finding your passion will change your life, too. Finding your passion will push you to dream big and act on those dreams. Finding your passion will inspire others to believe in you—maybe even more than you believe in yourself. Finding your passion will light a fire in your belly that will bring more joy and meaning to your life than any award or accomplishment.

When you find passion, your triumphs become so much more rewarding and your setbacks so much less daunting. Passion keeps you from boredom because it gives significance and purpose to your every moment. Following your passion is what separates those who live their dreams from those who can only dream.

Throughout your life, you've seen glimpses of the passion within you. Maybe it was a flash of comedic genius on a karaoke stage. Maybe it was an invention that came to you in your sleep. Maybe it was how much you enjoyed making friends in a foreign country. Maybe it was how you felt helping the victims of Hurricane Katrina. These flashes of meaningful purpose are commercials for the fulfillment that's possible when you look for, find, and then follow your passion.

Ben stumbled onto his passion when Leslie took him on a tour of the UN headquarters. He saw possibilities that he never before imagined. He chose to invest everything he had left—emotionally, financially, spiritually, and physically—to live that vision of connecting and empowering youth around the world. Choosing this path meant wading into the aftermath of civil wars, famine, disease, cultural battles, and other international issues most people choose to overlook. But Ben's passion had shown him what was possible and he was forever changed.

Finding and following your own passion separates you

from the millions of people with dreams but no drive. These are the people who harbor the most painful regrets as they grow old. They recognize what could have been but instead are prisoners of inaction. I know pursuing your passion won't make your life perfect, but I promise it will make it *unforgettable*.

Think about it this way:

- Your dreams show you what's possible.
- Deciding to live these dreams puts you in control.
- Finding the passion within you propels you toward your destiny.

BOUNCED: I'm just not motivated.

CASHED: My passion is my motivation.

WHAT BURNS INSIDE OF YOU?

In your Future Picture, you see yourself inspired, smiling, peaceful, creative, dedicated, and purposeful. What makes this picture so satisfying? The things you own? Your job title? Where you're living? How others see you? I don't think so. If you're truly inspired by the future you can create, it stems from something deeper and more personal.

This deeper motivation is the *why* behind your passion. This root of your most meaningful dreams might be a longing to make a difference, a longing to feel included, a longing to know your life means something, or a longing to know you lived life to the fullest. When you can see and name the why behind your passion, you gain the ability to take your passion to a new level.

The why behind Ben's unstoppable passion was his knowing how it felt to be abandoned, alone, hopeless, and beaten down. He knew what violence, drugs, poverty, and prejudice can do to the human spirit. He wanted young people around the world to rise above this pain to live their gifts. In helping young people find a meaningful path, Ben found his own.

Andi is another twentysomething who found her passion and used it to inspire a movement—albeit an artistic one. At twenty-seven, Andi had just quit her job and wanted to do something that really brought meaning to her life. She decided that more than anything she wanted to connect people in her city who would normally never talk, while creating an environment that fostered creativity and acceptance. Her solution: "Burn the Box"

For one evening a month, Andi arranged for a Realtor to donate the use of a very expensive house that was empty and for sale to showcase the work of local artists and musicians. Local businesses donated food and drinks, and all attendees made donations at the door that went to fund health care for the arts community. At these jam-packed underground events, it was common to see investment bankers talking politics, news, and art with blue-haired painters and nose-pierced college students. By bringing so many diverse people together, Andi not only revitalized her spirit but uplifted her entire community.

ASK YOURSELF WHY—THEN THINK WHY NOT

Are you still having trouble narrowing in on your passion? Speed up your search by answering these why questions:

1. What job would you do without pay for three years? Why?
2. Who is the person you would give everything you have to learn from Why?

3. Which one of your four snapshots could push you to work without sleep for days? Why?

4. How much time would you invest daily if I told you that it would take one thousand hours of learning and action to get exactly what you want? Why?

5. If you had to give away all your material possessions except one, which would you keep? Why?

6. What do you most want to experience in your lifetime? Why?

Now answer the big passion question:

7. Why is living your Future Picture critical to your very being?

_____

_____

If you had trouble answering the last question, you may need to redefine what you want from your life. When you are locked onto the right vision for your future, you will know why your life is important. By the way, don't worry if you can't find a direction that you are convinced will inspire you for the next forty years. That's a long time, and your view on what makes life so great will likely change. Instead, focus on finding a passion that will inspire you *this year*. After one year of feeling satisfied, it will be easier for you to make your next move.

BEGIN YOUR JOURNEY RIGHT NOW

Some people discover their passion only to feel so overwhelmed by all the work it will take to realize it that they procrastinate. To them I simply say this: One small step toward your passion is a giant leap toward making it a reality. So if you want to meet new people, join three volunteer organizations *to-*

day. When you get the opportunity, ask to lead one of their major volunteer projects. If you want to start your own business, call three entrepreneurs *today*. Ask them what they most love about owning their own business. If you want to live overseas, call three people *today* who can help you get there. Then go online and find out what types of employment or education opportunities exist in the country where you would like to live. By taking baby steps *today* that make your passion surface, you add urgency to living your Future Picture. This urgency inspires action, which leads to momentum, which leads to progress, which leads to—you guessed it—living your Future Picture.

DON'T TOSS IN YOUR TOWEL

For many of you, there may be the temptation to throw in the proverbial towel at the first hint of real-world resistance. This resistance could be as unexpected as getting into a car accident on the way to a big meeting or as common as panicking about making a major presentation in front of a room filled with important people.

Consider these real-world resistance scenarios:

- Would you go to night school so you could work, raise your kids, and complete your education?
- Would you try every day to convince strangers to donate their hard-earned money to some cause that you support?
- Would you start your own business knowing that you might go without a paycheck for a week, a month, even a year?
- Would you persist through dozens of rude rejections about your lack of talent in order to get your first big break?
- To live your dream, would you move to a country where your beliefs are in the minority?
- How much are you willing to risk to live out the dream in your heart?

The further your passion pushes you to live your dreams, the more likely you are to live them. Those of you who quit on your dreams before your dreams quit on you have reached your "Towel Point."

Your Towel Point is when your spirit quits on your dreams. This is the moment when your passion is defeated by the resistance you face. This is the moment when you start growing older but no closer to what you want. Your Towel Point marks the spot in time when you can stop trying *without feeling guilty*. You don't feel guilty because you believe you've given every ounce of effort that your dreams deserve.

Everyone has a Towel Point, but some people like Ben will never reach it. You can measure your Towel Point on the following scale of increasing real-world resistance. The more resistance you are willing to overcome to live the life you want, the more likely you are to get there.

To live your dreams would you be willing to

Towel Point 1: Read five how-to books in line with your passion in the next three months?

Towel Point 2: Adopt seven new actions, habits, or beliefs based on those books?

Towel Point 3: Ask eleven friends for help, support, and encouragement?

Towel Point 4: Share your dream with sixteen strangers who might be able to help?

Towel Point 5: Speak to a room full of skeptics about the importance of your vision?

Towel Point 6: Persist after twenty-two face-to-face rejections in public?

Towel Point 7: Borrow one year of your current pay or $50,000 (whichever is greater) to finance your dream?

Towel Point 8: Move to a foreign country where you and your beliefs are in the minority?

Towel Point 9: Sell all your personal possessions except one?

Towel Point 10: Not talk with your family or friends for one whole year?

Towel Point 11: Cut off all your options for retreat, so you have only one option: success?

What level would you go to on this scale before quitting on your most meaningful, powerful, personal dreams? Most people get to Point 4. That's a good start, because it allows for enough progress to get a sneak peek of what you're capable of achieving. However, if you're really dreaming big, you'll need to push yourself much further than Point 4 to get there. Remember, the bolder your dreams, the more resistance you will likely have to overcome to reach them.

SUCCESS IS RARELY A STRAIGHT LINE

Want to know the biggest enemy to your success that you can't see but is always with you? Self doubt. It whispers in your ear, creeps into your mind, and then spreads through your body— eventually turning your muscles into mush. And only one thing can conquer it. Passion.

Passion overrides self-doubt by spreading *from your heart to your head*. With passion fueling your resolve, you can go through, around, over, or under any obstacle to get where you want to be. In fact, each time your passion forces you to take a stand for your dreams you will feel more in control, alive, powerful, and resilient.

INSTANT MESSAGE

► Passion is inside you, but you must look for it to find it.

► Your *why* feeds your *will*, which leads you the right *way*.

► Refuse to throw in the towel, and move from spectator to participant to hero.

BOUNCED: I'm just not motivated.

CASHED: My passion is my motivation.

ONLINE: See awe-inspiring pictures from Global Youth Service Day at **www.myrealitycheckbounced.com/book**

4

UNLEASH OPPORTUNITY

> When you see opportunity, you see
> the future you can create.

REALITY-CHECK MOMENT—
I FEEL STUCK BUT I CAN'T SEE A WAY OUT.

For some twentysomethings, finding their Future Picture is
not the hard part—many have known what they wanted from
the time they were young or have a very clear, specific vision
for themselves. What's tough is when they achieve that Future
Picture, or fall short trying, and realize it's not what they
thought it would be. They become challenged, frustrated, lost,
and disenchanted. They have so blinded themselves to seeing
in only one direction that they can't see an escape route.

When Denise entered college, at age eighteen, she believed
she had only one option: take classes that would lead to a
high-paying job in business. She was the first and only one of
eighteen cousins to attend college, so big expectations rested
on her petite shoulders.

At first, she found her business classes interesting. But after
a few weeks, her mind was wandering in the ninety-minute
lectures. She got so bored, she began skipping classes to hang
out with friends. By the time she realized how far behind she

had fallen, it was too late to catch up. Her first-semester grades arrived by mail during Christmas break. When she saw her low GPA, she cried.

Feeling depressed and alone, she phoned her mom, Elida, at work. Elida listened patiently as Denise shared her frustration. She knew that Denise was smart. She knew that Denise was motivated when she wanted to be. She knew that Denise could have the world at her feet if she just figured out which way to step. So Elida told her eighteen-year-old baby girl that she was too talented to give up on herself. One bad semester should not sideswipe her entire future. She convinced Denise that maybe it wasn't college that was wrong for her, but rather studying business. She told Denise that one unexpected dead end doesn't mean other paths will turn out the same way.

TAKING A DETOUR

Denise listened to her mom's advice. Maybe she did need to try studying something else—even if it led to a lower paying job. The next day, Denise changed her *entire* schedule for the upcoming semester. She decided to enroll in a variety of classes, including ones she would never before have considered taking, until she found a direction that felt right.

The first class she took with this new attitude was about educating youth with disabilities. This class was as far from the College of Business as Denise could physically walk. She quickly learned that half her grade would be determined by a social service project. Twice a week for the whole semester, Denise would be required to volunteer at a school or nonprofit that served youth with disabilities. Denise and her friend Robert, a 240-pound linebacker, signed up to volunteer at the School for the Blind, the volunteer location closest to their college.

As her first volunteer day approached, Denise was anxious about helping kids who could not see. She was afraid it might be too much of a stretch for her skills and patience. After all, she had no experience helping blind people. She had no blind friends. In fact, *Denise had never met a blind person.*

Then she met Bobby, a thirteen-year-old-boy who was completely blind, had a speech impediment, and was mentally slower than other kids his age. Despite his challenges, he was full of spunk, and Denise liked him right away. She learned that she and Robert would work together on a project to help Bobby. She couldn't imagine what they could possibly teach him. Then she found out their assignment: bowling.

Yes, *bowling!* Apparently, Bobby had signed up to bowl in the Special Olympics, but he had never actually been bowling. It was up to Denise and Robert to teach Bobby how to bowl, something that neither of them were particularly good at— and they could see.

Denise didn't want to let Bobby down, but she had no idea how this was going to work.

The three of them held hands and, using a map, walked across the school's campus to a huge gymnasium. There, they went down a flight of stairs into a dark basement. Denise flicked the light switch and stopped in her tracks. The basement of the School for the Blind had a bowling alley! There were two regulation bowling lanes, racks of bowling balls, a scoreboard, and a machine that automatically reset the pins. Maybe blind bowling was more popular than she assumed?

Clueless on how to teach a blind kid to bowl, they started with the basics. First, Bobby had to learn the distance and layout of the lanes. To do this, the three of them walked back and forth down the lane from the foul line to the pins.

Robert then bowled one time so Bobby could hear the sound of his new sport. When the eight-pound ball collided with the old pins the explosive noise echoed around the concrete basement. Bobby smiled wildly. He wanted to make that sound!

The main difference between Bobby bowling and a sighted person bowling is that Bobby wouldn't be "throwing" the bowling ball. Instead, he would be placing the bowling ball atop a movable ramp located at the beginning of the bowling lane. He would then push the bowling ball down this ramp and it would roll toward the pins. The ramp moved side-to-side, so as Bobby got better he could aim for specific pins.

The main challenges for blind bowlers are learning how hard to push the bowling ball, how to aim to hit specific pins on the second roll, and then developing the patience to wait for the sweet sound of the ball and pins crashing together.

Denise helped Bobby position a six-pound bowling ball atop the bowling ramp. She stepped back while he pushed the bowling ball forward with all his thirteen-year-old might. The two of them stood motionless waiting for a sound. *Krrrraccc.cck!* Bobby hit the pins on his first try! Denise and Robert started cheering and clapping. At first Bobby froze, then he realized it was safe and began laughing and yelling and giggling.

Twice a week for a semester it went on like this. For three hours at a time, Denise and Robert would teach Bobby how to bowl. When Bobby had a particularly good practice session, the three friends would end their time together bouncing on a massive trampoline. They bounced until their legs felt like Jell-O. This must have been quite a sight: one full-grown linebacker, one petite woman, and one very happy thirteen-year-old, all bouncing together on a gigantic trampoline.

CHANGING DIRECTION

By the end of the semester, Denise saw a path that she had not allowed herself to see before. She realized helping kids made her heart dance. She transferred into the College of Education to become a science teacher. Since graduating college, she has taught science at an inner-city middle school, an affluent suburban junior high school, and now is a thirty-three-year-old principal in a rural school district. More than 30 percent of her students are in Special Education programs.

At night, Denise still pursues one opportunity she never imagined in her college days. The former business school student, who almost failed out of her first college semester, is now in the second year of a Ph.D. program. Her doctoral focus, fittingly, is on closing the achievement gap in public education. She wants to help kids from *all* backgrounds succeed—whether they bowl blind or are simply the first of eighteen cousins to go to college.

By opening her eyes to consider opportunities outside of business school, Denise discovered her Future Picture (see Chapter 2)—a career in education. She also found her passion (see Chapter 3)—that excitement and buzz you feel when you are living your true, authentic purpose. This rewarding career choice was always there, but at first Denise could not detect it. It took a bounced reality check to lead her to a thirteen-year-old blind bowler named Bobby who showed her what she was missing. By learning to experience the world through Bobby's perspective, Denise found her own path to meaning.

OPPORTUNITY SURROUNDS YOU

From the moment you hit the snooze button on your alarm clock to the hour you doze off watching late-night TV, opportunity is always around you. Opportunity is with you in your car on your morning commute. Opportunity is with you on your breaks during work when you call friends and family and surf the Internet. Opportunity is the seed that inspires your brief daydreams and long evenings gazing up at the stars.

Look around you now: The electricity that powers the stores near you was once *just an opportunity*. The computer you have come to rely on was once *just an opportunity*. The cell phone that never leaves your ear except to take pictures was once *just an opportunity*. So is the car you drive, country where you live, clothes you wear, music you enjoy, friends you make, places you travel, and memories you create.

When you recognize that opportunity doesn't come in one shape, size, color, degree, or last name, you can turn "randomly" bumping into a stranger at lunch into a lifelong friendship or maybe even your true love. You can convert a crazy invention that comes to you in the middle of the night into a thriving billion-dollar business. You can turn a single volunteer experience helping a blind kid learn to bowl into a lifelong calling. But to make these leaps of insight, innovation, courage, and meaning, you must first believe that opportunity exists all around you *all the time*.

Every second of your life contains the raw ingredients you need to seize an opportunity that will make your life more rewarding. If you disagree with me about the abundance of opportunity in the world, it's only because your mind currently keeps you from seeing it. When you learn how to teach your eyes to spot the opportunity in the world, you'll be shocked that you didn't see it before!

Like Denise, you might have a similarly blinding view of the opportunities available to you based on what you have personally or professionally experienced, what you have learned in school, and what friends and family have told you. Although some twentysomethings have known since they were eight years old what their calling is, you shouldn't feel confined to only one direction because you think that's the best you can do with what you have. This is absolutely the case if you are being pushed down a path that isn't making you feel happy, inspired, purposeful, and challenged. If you are willing to open yourself to the idea that there is an opportunity in the world that perfectly fits your personality and ambitions, your senses will adjust to reveal it.

OPPORTUNITY LESSON 1: BELIEVING IS SEEING

We all live on the same planet, but how you see the world is a personal, intimate choice. This individualized view of the world as you believe it to be is your perception, which is a result of your experiences, beliefs, and education. Your perception shapes how you see and interpret the world around you. Your perception is constantly deciding what you can and cannot view as an opportunity. Think about it like this: You are at a party with your friends, and each of you is deciding whether to go up and ask an attractive woman for her phone number. Some of you will look at the woman and say, "No way will she ever give me her number," and others will not be able to introduce themselves fast enough. Your perception of what's possible for you determines whether you have the courage to introduce yourself or if you'll stand alone against the wall looking lost.

Twenty-eight-year-old Alan knows how perception can either blind people to an opportunity or open their eyes to all its splendor. A friend approached him about a new biotechnology that makes protein glow and the possibility of turning it into a commercial venture—specifically, glowing fish. Alan was intrigued. Sure, the concept was way out there, but it did seem possible to him.

So Alan went to his family and friends to get their thoughts on the idea. Everyone he talked to about glowing fish told him flat out that he was crazy. A glowing fish would be cool to watch, but could someone actually create it? And if it were created wouldn't environmentalists keep it from ever reaching the market? And if it did ever make it to market, what kind of person would actually want to own a glowing fish? The more people told him he and his business partner were nuts, the more he began to sense what others could not: a glowing opportunity.

Oddly enough, the strongest encouragement came when his mom asked him to give up the crazy glowing fish nonsense. She reminded him he had a college degree and serious job offers. He didn't need to kill himself fighting a seemingly ridiculous uphill battle. Alan set out to make her proud by proving her wrong. He could see that if he and his business partner were able to make this idea work, the same challenges they faced would keep other entrepreneurs from copying their idea.

Four years after his mom told him to give up, Alan is CEO of GloFish, a successful company that is responsible for marketing the first biotech animal in the United States and Latin America—a truly glowing fish. He's been featured on pretty much every major media outlet and is now considered by many entrepreneurs as a visionary for biotech, someone who can find the glowing opportunities where others see only dead ends.

Like Alan, you can adjust your unique perception of the world to see opportunities that others may overlook or that you might not have allowed yourself to see before.

You've seen your unique perception in action if you've ever been in a heated argument about religion, politics, finances, ethics, or any other topic that touches on deep personal identity. The argument gets so intense because everyone involved, thanks to her unique perception, thinks she is absolutely right!

During the argument you might have thought to ask the

other person, "How in the world can you possibly think the way you do?" Wasn't the answer as obvious to her as it was in your mind? Yes! In fact, her answer was 100 percent as clear as yours, but it was still *different* from yours. This happened because, *through the other person's perception*, you were every bit as wrong as, from your own perception, you thought you were right!

You can always tell you've smashed into another person's perception of the world when she tells you, "Get real!" What she's actually saying is to step out of your perception of reality and *into hers*. If you did, then you would end up agreeing with her, because you'd both be seeing the world the same way.

Clashing perceptions can rip apart friends, families, even countries. Differing perceptions create conflict between people, because personal perception determines what you believe to be true and permits you to believe only evidence that reinforces your time-tested opinion. This happens because your super-powerful brain automatically adjusts what you smell, hear, taste, touch, and see to fit your deeper beliefs about what is right, wrong, and possible in the world.

Take the following perception pop quiz and see if your perceptions jibe with reality:

	(circle your answer)
How many gratifying jobs are available to you?	none / a few / lots
How many interesting people can you meet in one week?	none / a few / lots
How many successful businesses can you start?	none / a few / lots
How many people believe in you or would if you asked?	none / a few / lots

Here are the correct answers to the pop quiz: There are potentially *hundreds* of gratifying jobs available to you if you looked hard enough. There are potentially *dozens* and dozens of interesting people you could meet in only one week. There are *limitless* successful business that you could start. And there are *lots* of people who believe in you, or who would, if you only asked them to. The point of this pop quiz is to remind you that what you believe to be true about the world becomes what you perceive, which is then what you do your best to prove is right.

OPPORTUNITY LESSON 2: GET INTO THE PROPER MIND-SET

With time and practice, you can refine your perception to become virtual radar for discovering all sorts of opportunities. How so?

Start by telling yourself that opportunity is everywhere. When you have an opportunity state of mind, every problem is a possibility for greater achievement, every setback holds a secret to progress, every new contact puts you one person closer to your Future Picture. When you believe that opportunity is everywhere, this mind-set will build until it seems as if the entire world were working to help you live your dreams. This enables you to create spectacular success because, through your perception of abundant opportunity, it's *unavoidable.*

Once you believe opportunity is right around the corner, you will keep searching and trying new things until you find it. The more opportunity you uncover, the more opportunity you believe exists, the more options you have for getting where you want to go—and the faster you can choose to get there. With a perception of abundant opportunity, you can start life empty and end up completely fulfilled, because that's what looks and feels right to you.

The best example I recall of watching twentysomethings go from a perception of scarce opportunity to abundant opportunity happened when I was in college. We had a guest speaker who had retired from practicing law at age twenty-nine. He then won Entrepreneur of the Year for his new company at age thirty-four. After hearing the speaker's amazing life story, a classmate told the speaker that he, too, wanted to start his own business. The problem was he couldn't find a business concept that was proven to be successful. He asked the guest speaker how he came up with such a successful business concept so soon after retiring.

The guest speaker answered the class in a near whisper, "I have a thick book that lists almost every single company in business in our entire city. Not only does it list them, it also gives me a way to contact them."

Our class was shocked that such a book of successful businesses existed! The student immediately asked to borrow this prized book so he, too, could find these proven businesses and get started living his dream. Grinning, the guest speaker replied, "You already have this precious book, you call it the phonebook."

It turns out that our guest speaker hunted through the phonebook each year for business concepts to start. He looked to see which business sections were growing, which business sections were shrinking, and what business concepts looked promising. He then phoned the businesses he thought had the most potential and talked to their employees. He asked them how business was going, and they usually told him! This gave him a solid clue about whether to pursue the business concept further or move on to something else. I don't think anyone in our class ever looked at a phonebook the same way again.

BOUNCED: I don't see any opportunity to get what I want.

CASHED: Once I believe opportunity is everywhere, it appears!

CAN YOU SPOT OPPORTUNITY?

When you believe opportunity is everywhere, *the world becomes one big phonebook.* Consider whether you see the following four situations as great opportunities or time-consuming dead ends:

Situation 1: Twice a day on your commute you pass an abandoned, run-down house. It has a collapsing roof and you think people are dealing drugs there at night. You see a . . .

- dead end—an eyesore that should be condemned by the city and demolished.
- great opportunity—a house ripe for revitalization. Maybe you could turn it into government-subsidized housing or a homeless shelter.

Situation 2: You unexpectedly get fired from your first real job. You see a . . .

- dead end—worst thing that could have ever happened to you, because good jobs are practically impossible to find.
- great opportunity—permission and freedom to finally pursue your dream career.

Situation 3: You watch the evening news and learn that an overseas natural disaster has killed one hundred thousand people. You see a . . .

- dead end—another reason to stay home and change the channel.
- great opportunity—an undeniable call-to-action to get off your couch and start doing what you can to help the victims.

Situation 4: The stock market drops 20 percent in one year. You see a . . .

- dead end—take whatever money you have left out of the stock market and swear never to invest again!
- great opportunity—realize this type of market correction could be normal and might actually signal it's a great time to invest more money.

As these four situations show, opportunity is *always* right in front of you, but you must tune your senses to recognize it. You must choose to see beyond your physical surroundings and through your insecurities into what you can create. I call this mental state of heightened sensitivity to opportunity your Opportunity Radar. Three specific actions can help you create it:

1. **Coach yourself.**
2. **Apprentice yourself.**
3. **Challenge assumptions.**

Opportunity Radar Step 1: Coach Yourself— The Voice in Your Head Controls What You See

Admit it, you constantly talk to yourself. Sometimes you do this out loud in elevators and make strangers standing behind you feel uncomfortable. Sometimes you do it in front of the mirror to build up your self-esteem. But most of the time you carry on this nonstop internal conversation without ever making a sound or really even paying attention. This constant internal conversation is your commentary about the world and your place within it.

You can use this internal conversation to your advantage by *coaching yourself* to see opportunity. Start by inserting into your internal conversation thoughts about all the incredible opportunity that exists in the world. Tell yourself that a stranger sitting near you at a coffee shop might be the contact you need to open the door to a more rewarding career. Tell yourself that an empty storefront in a cute shopping center might be the perfect location for the boutique you've always dreamed about starting. By telling yourself that opportunity is camouflaged all around you *all* the time, you can begin to see opportunity in places and events where you normally wouldn't look.

Twenty-nine-year-old Rahul knows how coaching yourself for opportunity can dramatically change the course of your life. For three years, he managed fancy restaurants in hip cities such as Las Vegas. However, he always had a dream of one day becoming a professional golfer. Everyone who knew Rahul knew about his love of golf, but they also knew he didn't have the courage to make it a full-time career.

One evening a famous movie star was hanging out by himself in the restaurant Rahul managed. The celebrity invited Rahul to join him at his table. Their casual conversation turned into an intense two-hour discussion of why Rahul should leave his management job and chase his dream of playing professional golf. The celebrity told Rahul that the secret to living your dreams is reminding yourself every day where you are headed—and then following through. His advice to Rahul was to tell himself every day that he was going to be a professional golfer.

Rahul, twenty-eight at the time, took the advice to heart. After all, this movie star had achieved *his* dreams in his twenties. One month later, Rahul quit his management job and moved all the way to India to try to qualify for a professional golf tour. Now he is ranked in the top one hundred on the tour and he's been playing full-time for only one year! His morning ritual is reminding himself how much opportunity exists in the world and that he has the courage and talent to pursue it.

What you *repeatedly* tell yourself becomes what you think,

and what you think becomes what you believe, and what you believe becomes what your mind sees. When the voice in your head tells your eyes opportunity is everywhere, your eyes will adjust to see it so you can then live it.

This is why the best athletes in the world pay huge money to coaches, trainers, and psychologists. In the heat of battle, they want to make sure their biggest competitor is their opponent—not the voice in their head. You've seen this on TV if you've ever watched a professional football player yell into the air what he's going to do to the opposing team or a top-ranked tennis player talking himself up before he attempts a tie-breaking serve. This solo conversation moves you to a higher state of energy, focus, and performance.

If you want to find a better job, don't tell yourself, "There are no good jobs left" or "No one will ever hire me." Instead, tell yourself, "There are lots of good employers who are looking to hire someone just like me." The more you say this to yourself, the more you believe it, the harder you will work *to prove yourself right!*

If finding the right person for a long-term relationship is a priority for you, don't tell yourself, "All the good ones are taken" or "I'll never find the right person." Instead, tell yourself "The person I've been longing to meet is just waiting for me to introduce myself." The more you say this, the more you believe it, the more people you will *push yourself to meet!*

Coach yourself for opportunity and your mind becomes a radar, locating what you need to move ahead. You'll end up talking yourself straight into the future you desire.

To Coach Yourself into Opportunity:

1. Remind yourself every morning that you're a smart, confident, powerful person who attracts opportunity like a high-powered magnet.

2. If you don't see the opportunity you need, change your view. For example, if you want to start a business in your city but you can't find the right location, drive to another city and see what opportunity exists there. The same goes if you can't seem to find your true love in your local singles scene. Go to a new city or venue and meet new people there.

3. Whenever you are feeling trapped or stuck in a rut make a list of ten opportunities that you could pursue *today*.

Opportunity Radar Step 2: Apprentice Yourself— How Peer Pressure Can Improve Your Perception

You probably have felt the not-so-subtle pull of peer pressure at some point in your life. Peer pressure is powerful because it touches a very sensitive place: our human need to feel included, valued, and accepted by other people. As a result, you may change how you look, talk, or act just to make sure a particular group of people you want in your life keeps you in its circle.

Peer pressure is often viewed as a negative thing, but consider this: Used positively, it can actually be a powerfully motivating force. What if instead of surrounding yourself with people who encourage you to drink too much on weekends you surround yourself with people who push you to reach a higher level of success? In simple terms, by hanging out with people more accomplished than yourself you put yourself in position to have to conform to greater success. You're like a first-year athlete in the National Basketball Association (NBA). By playing at a higher level than you ever have had to before, you force yourself to improve dramatically just to keep up. This can be intimidating at first, until you see your peer group is still human just like you; but the pressure to conform will push you to succeed *much* sooner.

April can attest to the power of a peer group to put a person on the fast track in the real world. She was selected from applicants across her home state to work in Washington, D.C., for six months assisting a top legislator. It was an unpaid internship doing basic office work, but it forced her to constantly rub elbows with movers and shakers in D.C. politics. Each day on the job, she better understood the dynamics, language, and the way things get done within the Beltway. She incorporated these observations as quickly as she could to fit in. Six months later, she knew her way around the D.C. political scene. She still had no official power or formal authority, but you wouldn't know it from talking to her or watching her get things done.

When her six-month assignment was over, she applied for a full-time position with a federal agency. Her friends back home told her she would never get the job, because she lacked serious professional experience. But the people in D.C. whom she worked alongside told her that you never know until you try, so she submitted her résumé and landed an interview. In her interview with the hiring committee, she proved her D.C. prowess based on how she carried herself and the language she used. By applying what she learned keeping up with the best and brightest rising stars in the capital, she snagged a well-paid agency position *at age twenty-four!*

When you spend time, casually and professionally, with people who have achieved what you want, you pick up their words, mannerisms, ideas, and strategies. You start to see what they see, hear what they hear, and learn how to replicate what they do naturally. You start to understand why their world is full of opportunity *and how yours can be, too.*

To Apprentice Yourself into Opportunity:

1. Find out where people who are living a Future Picture similar to yours regularly hang out. Join their club, talk your

way into it, or keep sending them flowers (or adult beverages) until they invite you to join their table.

2. Volunteer at charity events where you can rub elbows with people who otherwise might be almost impossible to meet. When you get the chance, ask for their contact information and invite them to lunch.

3. Get involved with a civic organization that meets regularly to advance the success of their members, such as the Rotary. You can find a list of these organizations at www.myrealitycheckbounced.com/network

Opportunity Radar Step 3: Challenge Assumptions— Let the Facts Speak for Themselves

Banking on assumptions rather than facts is like rolling dice in the dark. Any bet on them is a fool's bet.

When you make decisions based on assumptions rather than taking time to get your facts straight, you're bound to make some poor choices. These might lead to minor setbacks or major defeats; but either way, they are avoidable. All you have to do to turn an incorrect and potentially costly assumption into a mistake you wisely avoided is to find out the facts *before* you jump to a conclusion.

When you make important decisions based on assumptions, you are setting yourself up to be caught off guard and unprepared. The farther you run with an incorrect assumption, the farther you will have to go back to fix it. I learned this lesson from Danny.

Danny was introduced to an entrepreneur who was making big money with an Internet-based business. This entrepreneur drove a fancy car, wore expensive clothes, and was always dropping names. Danny was told he, too, could make lots of easy money on the Internet if he simply got ten friends to join his "business" team. All he had to do was get these ten people to sign up and pay a registration fee. Danny would then receive a commission. Each person those ten people signed up would lead to another commission. Rushing into the opportunity, Danny immediately signed up his mom, dad, and close friends.

Two months later, the successful entrepreneur Danny trusted skipped town and took everyone's registration money with him. Danny then used Google to search for the guy's name and instantly found out that he was a serial con artist! In hindsight, all Danny had to do was a little bit of research, and he would have known the whole thing was a scam. Instead, he ran with an assumption that turned out to be incorrect and ended up burning himself, his family, his friends—and his reputation!

Assumptions aren't just bad when they lead to painful consequences; they can be equally bad if they blind you to a potentially great opportunity. When you assess opportunities based on assumptions rather than facts, you can easily overlook tremendous opportunity because you *assume* it's not there. This turns off your creative genius, so your attention moves elsewhere. You stop tinkering, looking, and exploring the potential opportunity from different angles. The result is that once you assume an opportunity doesn't exist, it no longer does—*for you.*

So how do you dodge incorrect assumptions that can lead to unnecessary pain and avoidable setbacks? How do you also know you've fully explored an opportunity before it becomes a missed opportunity? How can you find out whether you're living with assumptions *right now* that are keeping valuable opportunities out of reach? You cut through your assumptions by asking and answering direct questions.

Questions that demand facts separate incorrect assumptions from informed decisions. Before you even *consider* making a big decision based on an assumption, do the following:

1. **Ask specific questions.** If you're not sure about something, keep asking until you find out what you need to know. *Don't assume you know and think it's the same thing.* If the person you ask for answers is unsure, ask other people until you feel confident with the quality of the information you've gathered.

2. **Dig deeper.** Before you write off an opportunity as a time-consuming dead end, approach the opportunity from different angles. Sometimes the most rewarding opportunities are the ones other people have missed.

3. **Get a second opinion.** If you have no choice but to go ahead based on an assumption, get advice from people you trust *before* you take action. They may not have all the facts either, but they have wisdom that can help you make a more experienced decision.

With a Future Picture that motivates you to action you shouldn't be afraid to ask questions until you get the answers you need. It's much better to be teased for asking what seems to be a dumb question than to make an errant assumption that confirms you are dumb! I see it this way: If asking two or three questions can improve my chances of making the right decision, *I ask ten.* Questions lead to facts, and facts lead to good decisions. Good decisions lead to progress, and progress eventually gets you to your Future Picture.

WARNING: OPPORTUNITES ARE NOT CREATED EQUAL

Once you choose to see the world as overflowing with opportunity, you will find yourself inundated with new ideas and options. Now you face a different dilemma: separating the great opportunities from the mediocre ones. This is important because you have a limited amount of time to pursue opportunity, so you want to invest it where you can get the most value for your efforts.

To help you sort through opportunities to find the best one I've identified six questions you should ask. Together, these questions are the most *consistently effective* method I've found for separating golden opportunity from time-consuming distractions. These Six Questions of Opportunity are not always easy to answer. However, the answers will make it easy for you to decide whether to jump on an opportunity or keep looking.

THE SIX QUESTIONS OF OPPORTUNITY

Question 1: What specifically is the opportunity?

- Describe the opportunity in two different ways: once in a sentence and once in a paragraph.
- List other people, companies, and organizations that have taken advantage of this opportunity.
- Describe how you're different from them and similar to them and how you can use what they've already done to your advantage.
- Also consider: Is there a specific window of time for acting on this opportunity?

Question 2: What are the measurable outcomes from this opportunity?

- Describe what success in pursuing this opportunity would look like.
- Explain how you'll measure your progress pursuing this opportunity.
- Learn how other people measure their progress regarding this opportunity.
- Also consider: How many other people will get more joy out of their life if you succeed?

Question 3: Do these outcomes move you closer to your Future Picture?

- Compare your four snapshots to the outcomes that pursuing this opportunity is expected create.
- Do these outcomes align with your Future Picture? If the outcomes match, how long will it take for you to create them?
- Decide if this opportunity requires your constant leadership or if you can eventually pass the baton.
- Also consider: Is there a limit to how far you can take this opportunity?

Question 4: Are you passionate about this opportunity and its potential outcomes?

- Describe why you're passionate about this opportunity and its likely outcomes.
- Is your passion based on a short-term goal or lifelong desire?
- Calculate the amount of time you can invest daily toward this opportunity.
- Also consider: Do you have enough excitement about this opportunity to overcome the likely obstacles required to reach it?

Question 5: What resources do you need to act on this opportunity?

- Describe the tangible resources (such as money and contacts) and intangible abilities (resilience and public speaking, for example) that you will need to make the most of this opportunity.
- Determine if you have these resources and abilities or how you plan to acquire them.
- Determine whether you have the authority and time to bring these various resources together.
- Also consider: What must you prove or provide to get the resources you need?

Question 6: Who can help you research this opportunity and possibly play a role in pursuing it?

- Identify the roles necessary to pursuing this opportunity that you don't want or can't do.
- Determine who you know or who you could get to take on those roles.
- Decide how you could handle those responsibilities until the positions are filled.
- Also consider: Is there an organization that you could partner with to shortcut your path to this opportunity?

Answering the Six Questions for Opportunity may take a little work, but it enables you to weed out time-consuming distractions from the golden opportunities that deserve your full attention. Don't be disheartened if you have to consider many different opportunities before finding one that answers all six questions to your liking. Anyone can stumble onto a mediocre opportunity; but few have the patience, diligence, and wisdom to keep looking until they find an opportunity that warrants their complete attention.

As one of my mentors always says, "No deal is better than a bad deal."

He's a wizard at real estate, and his perfect thirty-year investment record speaks for the value of weighing opportunity. His philosophy is to consider a hundred real estate investments before investing his money in any one of them. Adding to his intense analysis of opportunity, he reinforces his Opportunity Radar through weekly meetings with financiers, bankers, brokers, politicians, and developers. These get-togethers help him keep tabs on the pulse of real estate currents and provide him with a sounding board for his investment decisions. He has not lost money in a real estate investment—*ever!*

OPPORTUNITY IS WITHIN REACH

Denise saw the opportunity she was missing by taking the risk to teach a blind kid to bowl. He showed her opportunity is more than what you can physically see—it's what you see *as possible*. Now, Denise helps an entire generation of kids learn how to see the world as overflowing with opportunity.

So when will you see the opportunities you've been waiting for and dreaming about? *As soon you believe they exist.* At that moment, you'll start to see past your surroundings and into what you can create!

INSTANT MESSAGE
► The world is overflowing with opportunity.
► When you believe opportunity is everywhere, you'll see it.
► Seeing an opportunity shows you what's possible for your future.

BOUNCED: I don't see any opportunity to get what I want.

CASHED: Once I believe opportunity is everywhere, it appears!

ONLINE: Learn what other opportunities Denise found at
www.myrealitycheckbounced.com/book

5

CAN YOU HEAR ME NOW?

> You never know who's sitting at
> the next table until you introduce
> yourself!

REALITY-CHECK MOMENT—
I JUST CAN'T DO THIS ALONE!

You can have all the talent, all the amazing ideas in the world, but if you don't know the right people, nothing happens. Doing it alone is *always* more difficult. That's why building a network of people who support you and your Future Picture— whether your next step involves finding a date, a job, a gym, or an apartment—makes your journey much easier. Many twenty-somethings mistakenly believe that building a powerful network from scratch requires going out and boldly meeting as many different people as they can. Sure, if you're a politician in the middle of a close election that may be a good game plan; but for where you're going, the *quality* of people in your network is much more important than the quantity.

To add quality people to your network, do what the most savvy power brokers do: Fine-tune the signals that you constantly send and receive so you attract the people you want. You can adjust your signals to always *draw a response* from people that moves you closer to your four snapshots. Think about it this way: Every quality person you add to your network brings with him his entire network. With the right people in your network you can get through to pretty much anyone imaginable.

Once you have mastered how to send and receive signals, you can then get through to virtually anyone whenever and wherever. This skill will come in handy whether you're eating french fries at McDonald's and see a hot guy you want to meet or sampling some fancy $10 appetizer at the Four Seasons and see a movie star you want to meet.

By the way, if you've never been to a Four Seasons Hotel— or a super-high-end hotel or restaurant in your area—I strongly suggest you put down your burger and go for a visit, if for nothing else than to watch networking pros in action. Where I live, in Austin, Texas, the Four Seasons Hotel is definitely *the* after-work hangout for the city's elite, elite hopefuls, and elite posers. This is networking central. Each weekday at about 5:30 P.M. the small tables in the rustic Lobby Lounge fill with wealthy hotel guests, celebrities, high-profile politicians, big-time dealmakers, and other assorted characters. I was twenty-one the first time I had a meeting in the Lounge.

I remember sitting in an oversize brown leather chair facing in the direction of a sharply dressed gentleman who had a loud laugh. He was at a table on the other side of the Lounge strategically facing the entrance. It was hard to miss the small sign prominently positioned on his table, which read "Reserved." His neat gray hair matched his understated but clearly expensive suit. I remember him because the group at my table was so entertained by his behavior. Whenever a person walked into the Lounge and looked around is if he or she were lost, the man would stand up and greet that person with a friendly hello. Then he would graciously offer him or her a seat at his table.

Most of the time those people politely declined in confusion; but by the end of my two-hour meeting, the gentleman had made friends with at least twenty complete strangers! This was even more amazing considering he showed up at the Lounge alone *and never left his table!* By the time I finished my meeting, so many people were sitting with him that the space their chairs occupied was twice the size of his reserved table. Everyone in his new group of friends was laughing, taking pictures, telling stories, and exchanging business cards. It was incredible.

This master of *plugging in* is Jerry Harris. The *Austin Business Journal* lists him as one of the city's ten most influential people. He's an attorney whom land developers rely on to help turn environmentally responsible projects into reality. Jerry introduced himself to me during my next meeting at the Lounge. He then invited me to sit at his famous table. We've been friends ever since.

In the many evenings Jerry and I have spent at the Four Seasons and community fund-raisers and just having lunch, he has never left without making at least five or ten new friends. Once we were talking in a small group at a large community fund-raiser. The event was absolutely packed. Across the room, Jerry somehow spotted a co-worker from twenty years before. Jerry waved the guy over, shook his hand, and asked how his four kids were doing *by name.* The guy couldn't believe Jerry remembered all his kids' names from twenty years earlier, but that's Jerry.

The "Mayor of the Four Seasons," as our local newspaper dubs him, is respected in Austin for always trying to help people. He does this by donating time to social causes and constantly thinking of who should meet whom. If you need your car fixed and call Jerry for a recommendation, he'll give you the names of three repair shops his friends own—and then he'll call each one of them on your behalf. He does this for old friends, new friends, and people he randomly meets at lunch.

One afternoon, Jerry and I were driving in his truck on a busy downtown street. He saw a friend walking on the sidewalk on the opposite side of the street. Jerry honked his horn, waved, shouted, and then circled *two blocks* just so he could stop the guy to say hi and wish him a good day. I laughed and shook my head. It was such a Jerry move. He just loves people. They give him the same enthusiasm in return.

Everywhere he goes, people say hello, shake his hand, take a moment to catch up or ask for advice, and show off the latest pictures of their family. The more people Jerry connects with, the more people he connects to each other. In doing this, he makes himself the center of an ever-expanding network. Building his network is more than something Jerry just does for work, it's his persona, and it's been the key to his remarkable success.

Imagine the relationships you would have if you applied Jerry's zeal for plugging in. You could create a network that truly *sets you up for life!* When you build this web of quality relationships, your connections grow and ultimately take on a life of their own. This leads you to eventually being able to make one phone call and *get whatever help you need anytime, anywhere.*

PLUG IN AND GET ENERGIZED!

The key to building your network is to *plug in.* This involves sending and receiving the right signals to attract the people you need. Learning to plug in gets you in the game and *keeps you there.*

Brandon, twenty-five, knows how plugging in can open all kinds of doors he never expected but always wanted. He had just finished grad school and wanted to live near the best night life in his city, which happened to be in the most expensive part of town. There were plenty of apartments available, but he wasn't making nearly enough money to afford one. Before completely losing hope, he told every one of his buddies about his wish and asked them to keep an ear open for any deals. As it turned out, one of these buddies happened to be in real estate and had heard that a new high-dollar condo was being built where Brandon wanted to live. The developer was in a financial bind, however. He needed to bring in some cash while the project was being completed, so he was going to rent the already-built condos for one year before putting them on the market.

When Brandon learned of this, he put on a suit and immediately went to talk with the manager of the condo project. He told the manager that he could move in the very next day and, if he were allowed to rent a condo, he would help recruit other responsible tenants. The manager and Brandon struck a deal: Brandon would attend one networking function on the condo management's behalf every week and in exchange he would get to rent a condo unit for $500 a month instead of the regular $1,750. Now that's plugging in!

When Brandon had to move out of the condo a year later, it sold for over $200,000. The entire year he lived there he only paid $500 a month in rent, and every time he recruited a new tenant, the condo managers *paid him!*

BOUNCED: I need to meet and greet as many people as possible to help me reach my Future Picture.

CASHED: I realize that plugging in with *quality* people makes reaching my Future Picture *much* easier.

THE SPOTLIGHT IS ON YOU

The challenge for you is learning how to plug in *now* so you always have, or can quickly make, the quality connections you need.

The best way to think about how to do this is from the perspective of the person you want to plug in with. Whether you realize it or not, people—from friends and family to strangers and co-workers—are always analyzing you. They are watching, noting, discussing, and remembering you and your actions. I'm not saying this to make you paranoid, but think about it: We all naturally do this to some degree. You may have done this by silently watching a girl at a coffee shop from a distance to see if she appears approachable. You may have done this by speculating with your co-workers about a new hire before you really get to know him. You may have done this assessing how difficult a professor will be before you finish your very first class. Based on your interpretation of the signals the person you're observing sends and receives, you make judgments about whether to try and talk to her, whether she is intelligent, whether she has money, maybe even if she is a potential threat. Based on all these signals you make a ton of assumptions that affect how you engage the person you're observing.

It's easy to overlook, but people are applying this same thought process toward you. They are doing it 24/7, 365 and it's time you sent and received the signals necessary to attract the people you want in your network.

You send and receive signals in two main ways: physically and verbally. You physically send and receive signals by the way you carry yourself, smile, laugh, listen, frown, cry, walk, shake hands, stand, make eye contact, dress and so on. You verbally send and receive signals by how you talk, ask questions, debate, joke, e-mail, instant message, interrupt, offend, gossip, profile yourself on a site like myspace.com, and so forth. To get plugged in and stay connected you must fine-tune your signals to match the Future Picture you desire.

To help you plug in using whatever network you have now, I've divided the remainder of this chapter into two sections:

- **Sending signals:** getting your message across
- **Receiving signals:** getting the message from others

Note: You may be wondering why I'm not using the word *communication* in this chapter. I'm avoiding that word like the plague because many people strongly link communication with talking. In truth, you send and receive *loads* of information without talking. By using the word *signal* throughout this chapter I help you keep in mind how much information you convey without ever making a sound.

SENDING SIGNALS

WORD UP

As a late-blooming teenager, I had the squeakiest voice known to any wannabe man. Whenever I answered the telephone with "Hello," the caller would always reply, "Yes Ma'am . . ." Ordering at a drive-through brought the same response. This was only slightly embarrassing, unless my friends were in the car cracking up at my expense.

These awkward adolescent exchanges had a huge effect on me. They taught me the incredible power of verbal signals. *What you say* and *how you say it* can make strangers immediately feel like family or repel them like a telephone solicitor.

Even if your voice does not crack like mine did at age

sixteen, improving your verbal signals will help you in our information society because *language* is the currency of information. If you can't send a signal that gets the response you want or need, you're as useful as fancy software that won't install on your computer. The software may have cost you a bundle, but it's of no value to you except as a paperweight.

To Send Verbal Signals That Get What You Want, Do Four Things

1. **Choose your words carefully.** In the English language there are approximately 961,958 words (according to languagemonitor.com). However, the average educated person has a vocabulary of about 14,000 words and uses about 2,000 in a week's conversation. This is why most newspapers are written on an eighth-grade level. They must appeal to the widest audience possible. This tells me that a good vocabulary is a competitive advantage. How? The more words you understand, the more resources you can turn to for educating and inspiring yourself.

At the same time, there are few things more embarrassing than having all eyes in a crowded room fixed on you as you are making a critical presentation—only to use an important word incorrectly. For the rest of your presentation, your one vocabulary booboo may be the single thing people think about and ultimately remember. To fill the void in your vocabulary caused by playing too many videogames and sending thousands of text messages on your cell phone, all you need to do is learn one new word each day. The new word doesn't have to be a huge word, just a word that you don't already know. The larger your vocabulary, the easier it will be for you to join any conversation.

TO PLUG IN: Join a monthly book club. This will get you in the habit of reading different kinds of books and discussing them in a group setting. A book club will also introduce you to new people who can take your network in unexpected directions. Subscribe to a word-a-day mailing list, like the one provided free from www.merriam-webster.com, and have a new vocabulary word delivered daily to your in box.

2. **Watch Your manners.** Nothing repels me faster than rude people. This includes people who are not rude directly to me, but those I see showing a lack of respect toward another human being. I want nothing to do with them. Rude people often can't see that disrespecting others only reveals their own lack of self-respect and maturity. Plus, they usually get what they give!

One of the most common mistakes young professionals make is being rude to people and co-workers who they think are low on the totem pole. Often the people with most menial jobs are also the ones most trusted in a company—they have keys to *every* office and can see the CEO whenever they want. Learn from those before you who ended up with egg on their face because of their arrogance. It's a mistake to be rude to people simply because they don't have a fancy title. You never know who they are related to, which boss they play cards with on weekends, or where else they might end up working.

You may be thinking, "But Jason, there's no way the tough, get-it-done leaders on the cover of big-time news magazines got there by always being polite." Sure, some of them are probably jerks, but the most successful leaders I know didn't get there by cursing at clients or slamming doors on little old ladies. In fact, the higher their profile, the more likely they are to mind their manners. Why? The media loves showcasing few things more than people whose power has gone to their head and eventually their head gets so big it falls off! Mind your manners, so when you make the cover of a magazine it has only good things to report.

TO PLUG IN: Think before you speak: If it would offend your mom's mom, don't say it. And definitely don't leave it on a voice mail!

3. **Perfect Your presentation.** My college career adviser told me that I had to have a great thirty-second commercial about myself. This was in case I got into an elevator with someone I wanted to impress. Although this is excellent advice, I have rarely found myself with thirty uninterrupted seconds to talk with a bigwig I didn't know beforehand.

Instead, I found that at best I had ten seconds, approximately two to three sentences, to grab the other person's attention. If I could successfully do this, then I could open the door to talking with him for much longer. Those all-important first sentences became my IM—introductory message. Having two or three great sentences ready to go makes it easier for me to start conversations with anyone, anywhere.

You'd be wise to create your own IM, so you always have a few great opening lines ready for making new, important contacts. Having a few polished introductory sentences shows you are confident, intriguing, intelligent, and memorable. It also makes it easier to get the other person's contact information. She can see you're worth talking to again. To create your own IM, consider what you have to say that would interest other people. Don't just tell them how great you think you are or how much you know. Instead, tell them only enough so that they are intrigued and ask to hear more. Comedy and similarity can be good conversation starters, too, but if you're not funny don't introduce yourself with a joke. The other person may think you're the punch line! Lead with your well-rehearsed IM, and you can turn any stranger into your new hottest contact.

Twenty-six-year-old Sonya knows about IMs—good and bad. She is a bartender at a popular night club. Over the years she's heard so many cheesy pickup lines—which are really a form of introductory message—that she and her friends have started writing down the worst ones:

- I'm rich, I'm bored, and my mom would approve of you.
- Is your dad a thief? Because he stole the stars and put them in your eyes.
- Your shirt would go great on my carpet.
- Are you from Tennessee? Because you're the only ten I see.

TO PLUG IN: Write down twenty-five potentially great opening lines that could serve as your all-important introductory message. Narrow them down to your five favorites. Call three friends whom you respect and ask them which of the five opening lines best introduces you, your strengths, and your ambitions.

Here are three IMs I might use, depending on the situation:

Example 1: My name is Jason. I write books. [The ultimate coffee shop pick-up line.]

Example 2: My name is Jason. I own a company that helps people get good jobs.

Example 3: My name is Jason. I help people get back on their feet when life knocks them down.

4. **Go beep yourself.** Cell phones seem as if they have become an extra body part. I hear people talking on them during dinner, in the middle of movies, and even in the bathroom! In fact, I know only one twentysomething who doesn't have a cell phone. Instead, he has *two*, which he carries with him at all times: one for personal phone calls and one for business phone calls. Even my little sister in middle school is on her second cell phone!

All this reliance on cell phones makes your voice-mail greeting the first contact point for many people trying to reach you. This raises the importance of this recorded greeting, because you never know who might be calling. It could be friends from college, your grandma, a banker, or a potential employer.

My friend Jake knows the power of voice mail, because his ex-girlfriend used it against him. When they broke up she changed his work voice-mail greeting to something totally offensive. It took him a full day to figure out why he wasn't getting any messages at work. When a friend finally clued him in to the offensive voice-mail greeting, he was *really* embarrassed. He doesn't know how many calls he missed because of the insulting greeting. However, he does vow to never again tell a girlfriend his password!

Another friend of mine, Angela, had a pretty typical voice-mail greeting that simply said, "This is Angela. Leave me a message." I suggested she make it a little more upbeat and professional because she was in the middle of a job search and using her cell phone as her contact phone number. She changed her greeting to, "This is Angela. I'm sorry I can't personally answer your phone call. Please leave me a message and I will call you back. Thanks!" She was shocked when her old friends kept leaving her messages saying how much they liked her new greeting. Until her friends reacted so strongly, she never imagined how much effect a simple recorded greeting could have.

When it comes to recording your voice-mail greeting—work, home, or cell—be creative but safe. Something professional like Angela's message is one way to go or you could make it a little more fun and personalized. Just be sure you record it in a quiet area so they don't hear Metallica playing in the background! The same forethought is important when leaving messages on other people's voice mail. Many employers save *all* voice mails (and e-mails) that their employees receive. These can be used against you when you least expect it. Don't get caught sounding like a fool on tape; think before you leave your message so the recipient gets the right signal no matter how many times they play it back.

TO PLUG IN: Change your voice-mail greeting every two months.

IMAGE IMPROVER

Image is the bundle of signals your physical *actions* and *presence* send into the world. Image is important because the way people see you influences how they initially treat you. With the right image, you can open up doors before you even open up your mouth.

And trust me, no matter what jeans you wear people notice you. When you walk into a crowded room, they check you out from head to toe. They make assumptions (right or wrong) about who you are without taking the time to actually get to know you.

This habit of people sizing you up and fitting you into a category can make or break your chances of impressing them before you get the chance to use your IM. If your image doesn't match the Future Picture you desire, the people you need on your side may never give you a chance to reach the opportunities you need. However, you can choose to use this "judge them before you know them" habit to your advantage by crafting an image that attracts and motivates people to *want to* meet you and support your efforts. Focus your image on your strengths. Do this by thinking outside in rather than inside out.

To Send a Physical Signal That Gets What You Want, Do These Four Things

1. **Keep your head up.** People pay attention to how you carry yourself. When you walk is your head up and confident or are you slouching and looking worn out? This one simple habit re-

veals much about your attitude. People meeting you for the first time may go so far as to interpret how you carry yourself as evidence of *how you might carry them* in a time of need. Think about it: Do you want the person with the firm handshake who holds her head high on *your* team or your *opponent's*? I want her on my team!

Have you ever met a new person who introduces himself with a limp-fish handshake while looking at his feet and mumbling his name? I have. It sure doesn't send a message of confidence and leadership. Instead, it sends a message of anxiety and insecurity, exactly what you *don't* want to convey when trying to get plugged in. Get your image off on the right foot by always offering a firm handshake, making good eye contact, and having decent posture. This goes whether you are a man or a woman, going for a job interview or on a blind date.

Jose, twenty-two, was raised in an area of the South where it was considered disrespectful to look your elders in the eye. He strictly adhered to this policy until he went away to college. There he quickly learned that unless he did look people in the eye, they didn't trust him. He admits he still has issues making eye contact with his older relatives; but he says that since he started looking people in the eye, his college dating life has definitely improved!

TO PLUG IN: Before you go into a meeting or on a date, take a deep breath, collect your thoughts, and then walk in with confidence.

2 **Dress the part**. Your clothing, jewelry, hair, accessories, makeup, and so on form the billboard that presents your physical message to the world. What message does your billboard sell? Do you wear low-cut shirts that make people notice your body instead of your brains? Do you wear pants so low that your boxers are on display? Is your hair purple and your nose pierced?

None of these is wrong. In fact, I like purple hair. Still, all these choices are part of your physical billboard, which sends a signal that can make certain Future Pictures more difficult to achieve. Unless a potential boyfriend or employer takes the time to get to know what a great person you are on the inside—and that you just happen to really like the color purple—he may never see beyond what's on your outside. Instead, he may look at you from a distance, assume he know's your "type," and dismiss you based on your physical appearance alone. I know you may be saying to yourself, "Who cares if he doesn't like me because of the way I choose to look? I don't want a person who stereotypes in my life anyway." I understand; I had hair down to my shoulders during college. *All* I am saying is to be aware of the signal your physical appearance sends to the world and consider adjusting it, when necessary, to align with your Future Picture. In other words: If you're going on a job interview, wear clothes that show you mean business. If you're going to the beach with friends, wear the tiniest bikini you want. Just know that *the part you dress for is often the part you get.*

TO PLUG IN: If you can't afford professional clothes for an important job interview, borrow them from a friend or buy them secondhand. No one will know but you. When you get the job you'll be the one laughing all the way to the clothing store of your choice!

3. **Leave a paper trail.** Your physical appearance leaves the room when you do. What connects the people you have just plugged in with back to you? What are the breadcrumbs you leave behind for your new, important contacts to reach you later? Your paper trail is your networking bread crumbs. This is the printed material that you leave behind, or send out, that displays your name, image, and contact information. This includes your business cards, letterhead, envelopes, and Web site

(if you have one), and even the address of your myspace.com page.

Everyone, whether she lives with her parents, has her dream job, is attending college, is currently unemployed, or just has big dreams that she needs help to reach should have:

- Professional-looking business cards
- Matching letterhead and envelopes (stationery)
- Politically neutral e-mail address

This may seem like overkill if you are a freshman in your first semester of college, but trust me, looking good on paper says lots about you and how you see yourself in the future.

I'm making a point of this, because I meet so many twentysomething professionals and aspiring professionals whose paper trail is simply not up to par with their ambitions. I've met third-year teachers who won't get business cards because they think, "I'm just a teacher." I've even met doctors who write notes to patients only on the letterhead they get for free from pharmaceutical companies.

How would you feel knowing that your teacher, or your kid's teacher, doesn't take himself seriously enough to get his own business card? Or that your highly paid and highly skilled doctor won't spend two cents to write you a holiday note on her own stationery? You have to wonder if these people are just lazy or if they don't realize how important they are to the people they serve. If you're a professional, or simply on a path that becomes easier with the more quality people you have in your network, put your professionalism in writing! *Every* piece of paper that you leave behind that connects people back to you represents you. For a small amount of effort and very little money you can create a paper trail that your new contacts will want to follow.

TO PLUG IN: Invest $50 in your future. Buy some decent letterhead and envelopes. Print five hundred sharp-looking business cards. You can get all these at your local copy store office-supply store, or print shop. Then keep in mind that your fancy business cards do you no good if they remain in your pocket! If you really want to secure your image, buy your name as a URL address—before someone else does! (see jasondorsey.com)

4. **Keep it clean.** As we get older it seems we all accumulate stuff. How you organize and maintain your stuff says a lot about who you are and what you most value. By taking a few minutes each week to keep your three main spaces in order— home, office, and car—you show the outside world that you take care of your business. This makes other people more willing to trust you with theirs.

I learned this lesson the hard way when one of my mentors asked for a ride to his office after our lunch meeting. The entire time we were driving he was giving me "constructive criticism" about what a mess the backseat of my car was. At the time, it was covered in books, boxes, mail, and folders. He said with a backseat like that I shouldn't need an office! I took the hint and cleaned up my act. Stay organized. That way you inspire trust and can keep track of your progress.

TO PLUG IN: Every Friday, set aside twenty minutes to organize the space in which you spend the most time: home, office, or car.

RECEIVING SIGNALS

READING BETWEEN THE LINES

I bet that *at least once* you've been in the uncomfortable position of incorrectly interpreting another person's signals to you. When this happens, you wind up at the wrong location for an appointment, you think someone is flirting with you when really she's just being nice, or you get offended when no disrespect was intended.

Getting your wires crossed always leads to stress—even if it's for only a short time—until someone straightens things out. To make sure you avoid this unnecessary stress and get the message right *the first time*, learn to become a world-class signal receiver.

To Receive the Right Information, that Allows to You to Make the Right Response, Do These Four Things

1. **Keep your ears open.** The fastest way to make a new friend or turn your enemies into allies is to *actually* listen to what they are saying. This is different from hearing someone's words and nodding along while you glance around the room and wish you were talking to someone else. Actually listening requires paying attention to what the other person says and how he says it. All these signals add up to you getting his point the way he intended.

   The easiest way to actually listen, instead of only halfway hear, is by adding three simple habits to your plugging-in conversations.

   Habit 1: Allow the other person to make her key points without interruption.

   Habit 2: Summarize her major points back to her. (So I think what you are saying is . . .)

   Habit 3: Ask a specific question or two about her main point.

These three habits are so simple, but most people won't add them to their conversations, no matter how important the new contact. The reason is simple: Most people would rather hear themselves talk than really listen to someone else! As a result, they miss out on valuable information and a more meaningful connection that could open the door to otherwise unreachable opportunity.

TO PLUG IN: When you meet a new person, say his name three times during the conversation and you will remember it.

2. **Say it ain't so.** Even if you're the nicest person in the world, you're going to have conflicts, debates, arguments, and disagreements. These verbal sparring matches test your critical thinking skills and help you refine your view of the world. They also allow you a chance to spread your opinions and work out new solutions to difficult problems.

When you're in a disagreement, go into it clear about your *intentions*. You can argue to prove yourself right (winning for your ego) or you can argue to learn (so your path ahead becomes easier). If your goal is simply to prove yourself right, you may leave the argument as the victor but not necessarily any wiser. If your goal is to be better informed than when you started, you may not always win the verbal battle but you will be better prepared to win the war.

Whatever your intentions, to effectively represent your side in a disagreement, you must know how to listen to the other person's view. When you listen to the other person's view, you put her in a position in which she has to listen to yours. If she doesn't, she automatically appears small-minded and hardheaded, which takes away from her credibility. In doing this, you also force her to listen to your side of the argument which gives you a chance to persuade her of your reasoning. Best of all, when you make the effort to understand the other person's perspective you are heightening your senses to find the weak links in her argument.

If you want to *really* position yourself to come out on top in an argument, send the signal that you value the other person's opinion *so much* that you need to carefully consider it. Then go ahead and make the decision that fits what you believe to be true. By showing that you seriously considered her view, you are more likely to leave an unsettled argument not as enemies but as adults who are mature enough to agree to disagree.

TO PLUG IN: If your argument is getting too heated and you need to slow it down, take out a piece of paper and with the help of the other person write down point by point what you're disagreeing on and why.

3. **Be the meeting master.** Meetings are a necessary but time-consuming part of life whether the meeting involves three people or three hundred. This is true if you're in grad school, working at a *Fortune* 500 company, or planning your wedding. So when it's your turn to host a meeting, set yourself up to receive major kudos as a meeting master. You do this by keeping the meeting fun, focused, inclusive, and outcome driven.

To be a meeting master
- Decide on a few simple ground rules *before* you start the meeting. This gives everyone equal footing and gets the meeting off to a positive start.
- Share the meeting's agenda with all participants in advance. This gets everyone on the same page and makes the desired outcomes clear from the beginning.
- Allow meeting participants to offer changes to the agenda, as long as they do so in advance. Also assign premeeting responsibilities as necessary. These could include taking notes, bringing food, and securing a meeting place.
- Have some visual reinforcement that keeps the meeting's bigger mission in focus. This could be a picture, quote, memento, book, or handout.
- Move the meeting along at a good pace. If someone is monopolizing the conversation or adding interesting but

unnecessary facts, be the one who politely gets the meeting
back on track.
• Before the meeting concludes, get clear on next steps,
timelines, and individual commitments. Depending on the
purpose of the meeting, you may want one person to e-mail
the commitments and corresponding timeline to all
attendees afterward.

Leading a meeting gives you the chance to show your leadership skills. Listen to what people say, guide healthy debate, and
keep the meeting moving forward. Remember, *she who sets the
agenda has the power.*

TO PLUG IN: Step up and offer to lead a meeting for your
group or organization.

4. **Be true to your word.** There is no bond as important, or as fragile,
as the commitments you make. If you couldn't make and keep
commitments, you wouldn't be able to borrow money from a
bank, marry your true love, or be part of a functioning government. Thank goodness you get to be half of a commitment!

How well you keep your commitments establishes your
reputation. If you're a twentysomething, you have a long road
ahead. Get a bad reputation early and you add more challenges to your drive toward your Future Picture. Send a clear
signal to the world that you can be trusted and accountable by
keeping *all* the commitments you make.

This includes those teeny, tiny commitments you sometimes undervalue, such as being on time to meet friends, paying your credit-card bills, and remembering an anniversary. If
you're ever in doubt whether to make a commitment, remember: It's always better to underpromise and overdeliver than to
overpromise and underdeliver.

The worth of your handshake shows how you live your life.

TO PLUG IN: If you're not sure you can keep a commitment, let the other person know in advance. This way he can make any necessary preparations.

IMAGE IMPROVER

How you physically receive the signals that other people send to you tells them how they should respond next. You know what I'm talking about if you've ever seen your boss smirk before answering when you ask for a promotion, seen your parents laugh when you ask for money, or someone move closer to where you're sitting after you make eye contact.

How you react physically to the messages other people send your way can be so revealing that the other person doesn't need to hear your verbal response. Based on your physical reaction *alone* he can sense what you're going to say before you say it. All the more reason you must think, not only before you act *but before you react.*

To Physically Receive Information from Other People so You Stay Plugged In, Do These Three Things

1. **Face the truth.** As you listen to other people, your face and body naturally respond to what you're hearing. These physical expressions suggest to others whether you believe them, disagree with them, are interested in them, or just want to ignore them. You send all these revealing signals without opening your mouth (unless you're yawning). It's amazing that the look on your face can say so much about what you're thinking *while you're still thinking.* Your reaction to other people's signals is virtually written from cheek to cheek.

   It may be easier to think about how you physically receive information by reversing the situation: If you're talking with someone and she keeps looking around the room, what does that say about her feelings toward you? Not interested or maybe nervous. If you're talking with someone and he rolls his eyes, what does that say about what he is thinking? Yeah, right or possibly no way. If you're talking with someone and she raise's one eyebrow, what does that imply? That she is shocked or possibly skeptical.

By learning to pay attention to your expressions *while you're listening*, you can subtly take control of a conversation. Prove this to yourself by listening to one of your friends tell a story and respond to the story with unexpected facial expressions. When he says something positive give him a look of sadness, when he says something negative pretend you're happy. When you have counterintuitive reactions to his story he won't know what to do except look confused! You took control of the conversation without ever saying a word.

This is also where the shock factor comes into play. When someone makes you an offer you don't like, the more shocked and outraged you appear physically, the more uncomfortable *she* become's. Try this next time someone says something that offends you; it can be hilarious. The opposite is also true. The more natural you appear receiving an offer, the more natural the other person feels making the offer.

TO PLUG IN: Next time someone tries to sell you something in person, pay close attention to your facial and body language. The less interested you appear physically, the faster he will lose interest in you!

2. Proofread.

Dear Harvard Admissions,

In considering my application for admission, you should know that I've wanted to attend Harvard since I was a little kid. I have had Harvard posters on my wall since second grade. I know that my academic achievements reflect my potential

for success at your fine institution. Crimson is my color and
VE RI TAS is my T-shirt! For these reasons and many more
you can see why Stanford is the right place for me.

What?? A one-word typo just made an admissions committee chuckle. They gave someone the opportunity to apply to
their school, and she accepted this opportunity without
proofreading her application. This type of thing happens
more often than you think because many people use the same
essay for completing multiple college applications.

Similar typos in written replies occur all the time, professionally and personally. These errors show readers that you're
not paying full attention to them. I remember, when I was
a teenager, I sent a thank-you card to someone who helped
me get a job. He was kind enough to take a red pen to my
note and send it back to me—*corrected!* From then on, I read
my written replies out loud and haven't trusted spell check to
save me.

When you reply to someone in writing, nothing makes you
look sillier than errors confusing write and wrong. Take your
time and get it write.

TO PLUG IN: Before you send an important written message,
get a friend to proofread it.

3. **Be a welcome mat.** With all the traveling I do, I end up eating
   alone at least three or four meals a week. After nine years of
   life on the road, eating alone is pretty much second nature to
   me. I usually bring a newspaper to read or sit back and watch
   the locals come and go. As accustomed to eating alone as I am,
   it's always nice to visit a new restaurant in a new city and have
   a local introduce himself.

   These human welcome mats are the best public relations
   people a city can have. By showing solo travelers a little hospi-

tality, they make their entire city feel more inviting. They can turn a silent meal into a memorable conversation. They also can recommend places to visit off the beaten path as well as well-traveled places to definitely avoid.

When I'm home in Austin, I try to be one of these welcome mats. If people are lost, I give them directions. If someone is sitting alone at a social place, I try to talk to her. When you're friendly, you never know who you'll meet.

Once I was in line at a lunch buffet and wound up helping a little kid in front of me scoop some potatoes onto his plate. His dad saw this and came over. He thanked me for helping his son and asked if I wanted to have lunch with them. I was alone, so I quickly accepted. I had a nice lunch with their family, and as I was leaving, the kid's dad gave me his business card. He said to call him if I ever visited their hometown. Until I read his business card, I had no idea the kid's dad was CEO of a multi-*billion*-dollar company. I was just trying to help the little kid get some potatoes.

You never know who's sitting next to you until you introduce yourself. Or until he invites you over and you're brave enough to accept!

TO PLUG IN: When you see a person sitting alone at lunch, invite him to join your table.

PLUG IN AND GO!

I learned or refined all the strategies and actions in this chapter on plugging in from many afternoons and evenings hanging out with Jerry Harris. He's called the Mayor of the Four Seasons for good reason. He listens to people so well that he makes friends *everywhere* he goes. He asks good questions, keeps the conversation lively, and always invites strangers to his table. Strangers such as a wide-eyed, twenty-one-year-old kid who became a much better person for knowing him and learning from him.

By this point you're probably asking yourself, "Okay, now that I know how to plug in, *who in the world* should I try to connect with first? And how do I spot the people I need to help me make my Future Picture come true?" Fret not, the answer to those questions begins in the next chapter.

INSTANT MESSAGE

► The signals you send and receive determine how well you connect.

► Once you learn to plug in, you can build a global network starting right where you are.

► When you're fully plugged in you can make one call and get what you need!

BOUNCED: I need to meet and greet as many people as possible to help me reach my Future Picture.

CASHED: I realize that plugging in with *quality* people makes reaching my Future Picture *much* easier.

ONLINE: Read more about Jerry's networking adventures at **www.myrealitycheckbounced.com/book**

6

SECRETS TO BUILDING YOUR REAL-WORLD DREAM TEAM

It's not who you know, it's who you can *count on* that matters.

REALITY-CHECK MOMENT—
BUT I DON'T KNOW THE RIGHT PEOPLE.

In the last chapter, I showed you that you can't succeed all by your lonesome and that building a tag team is essential to realizing your real-life dreams. Your next challenge is to figure out how to get the best and the brightest stars on your team. Before you throw up your hands in "I have no famous contacts" defeat or complain that this person is successful only because her rich daddy helped her or that person is connected only because he went to the right private school, recognize *you* can assemble the star power you need in your network. All you have to do is plug in *strategically* and you can get the quality people you need on your side. But where do you go to find those people?

Approaching his graduation from law school, Jimmy found himself mired in over $100,000 of debt. He had dreams of one day establishing his own law firm, landing his own clients, calling his own plays, and creating an international reputation; but at the moment, Jimmy was just a broke, soon-to-be law school graduate with a C– average. What's more, he had a total of zero connections in the city where he wanted to live.

Jimmy's future was very much up in the air. He knew he wasn't cut out for the traditional big-law-firm, pay-your-dues path. He didn't want to work eighty hours a week in a cubicle hoping to politic his way to partner in ten years. He also knew he wasn't the type of person who could work long hours at the DA's office or laboring on painstaking research to write briefs for a judge. He burned to star in high-profile cases in packed courtrooms. He dreamed of winning life-altering verdicts that hinged on his ability to persuade a jury; but right now he'd feel lucky if he could get *any* job offer.

LAW AND MENTOR

Jimmy's fortunes changed on a rainy day in 2001. One of his law professors instructed him to attend a trial in which Dan Cogdell, a famous criminal defense attorney, flamboyantly defended an investment banker accused of killing his wife. Jimmy was amazed at how Dan defended his client and ultimately earned an acquittal.

Sitting in the back of the courtroom, Jimmy saw his future. Dan was the person who could teach him how to defend clients facing the death penalty. Dan could teach him how to build his own law firm. Dan could teach him the wisdom that comes from winning big and losing publicly. Jimmy knew that with Dan's help, he could escape the years of drudgery it typically takes for new attorneys to make a name for themselves.

Jimmy also knew that such a high-profile attorney would not be easily motivated to meet with, let alone help, a C– law school student. Jimmy had to plug in and do so *wisely*.

He began by contacting anyone he could think of who might know Dan. He talked to his law school professors and anyone else who might know someone who knew someone who knew Dan. One night, Jimmy shared his intentions with a bouncer outside a popular dance club. Of all people, this bouncer knew Dan.

The bouncer arranged a twenty-minute meeting for Jimmy with Dan at a low-key Chinese restaurant. Jimmy prepared for the meeting as if he were going to court. He worked on a good introductory message; arrived early; and was as polished, professional, and ambitious as he could present himself. Dan listened and watched. Something about Jimmy reminded him of himself. Maybe it was his intense desire. Maybe it was his bluntness. Maybe it was his distaste for kissing butt at big law firms. Maybe it was his persistence in trying to meet with him. Whatever it was, Dan decided to take a calculated risk to find out more.

He offered Jimmy a chance, *one chance*, to prove what he was made of: Jimmy could work at Dan's firm for a set period of time doing whatever legal work, no matter how menial, that Dan assigned. Dan would then evaluate Jimmy on the quality of his work and his work ethic to see whether he was all talk or a trial lawyer in the making.

Jimmy spent two years—including his entire last year of law school—working long hours for Dan. He proved his talent, but Dan knew talent needed more than a predictable paycheck to blossom. So, he made Jimmy only one offer of employment. Jimmy could take it or leave it. The offer was: Jimmy could have an office in Dan's boutique criminal defense firm and Dan would refer work and cases as he saw fit. In exchange, Jimmy would receive no set salary, but he would be paid hourly for the cases Dan sent him. The upside was that Jimmy would be free—*and expected*—to build his own legal practice as best he could. The downside: Jimmy would have to get his own clients, argue his own cases, and collect his own fees if he was to make it and to do all this with no experience as the lead attorney in a courtroom.

Dan's employment offer was exactly *opposite* of those sought by Jimmy's high-achieving classmates. All they cared about was their signing bonus, guaranteed first-year salary, the average years to make partner, and a firm's name. They knew they were going to slave away doing research and pushing paper for a few years, so the salary soothed their pain.

If Jimmy accepted this "find out what you're made of" offer, his back would be against the wall. His $100,000 education loan was about to come due. He had little savings to cover his apartment, truck, and other living expenses. He also had no money for the marketing necessary to land the initial clients that would lead to more clients.

This was the test. Did twenty-six-year-old Jimmy believe in his dream enough to put his entire legal career in his own hands?

LEGAL JEOPARDY

Five months after agreeing to this sink-or-swim offer, Jimmy learned that he had passed the Texas bar examination on his first try. That same afternoon, he visited offices, restaurants, and social gatherings to hand out his hot-off-the-press business cards. He then hit the phone, contacting former classmates, family friends, entrepreneurs, and anyone else he could possibly think of who might know people who could use a criminal defense attorney. To get clients fast, Jimmy became a networking machine.

It wasn't enough. After one month, Jimmy could see he

didn't have the contacts to get the referrals he needed to launch his legal career. He had an amazing mentor to guide him in the practice of law, but he needed other influential people to refer the clients that would get him into the courtroom. What Jimmy needed was a *tag team*. A group of people so committed to his success, that they invest their time, talent, and contacts without expecting anything in return.

Jimmy stepped back from his furious card-slinging sprint and studied the social, political, and business power structure of Houston. He researched to find out who really had the influence. He then made cold calls and otherwise creatively plugged in to reach those key power people. He then offered them lunch, coffee, and any other reason he could think up for getting together.

It takes only one meeting with Jimmy to see his passion for criminal defense. The people he strategically plugged in with saw the fire in his belly. They also commented on the credibility Jimmy gained by having such a well-known mentor. Slowly, a few big shots in the community sent over a friend or two who needed legal help. It was a test to see if Jimmy knew what he was doing. With each case Jimmy successfully resolved, he was sent more cases. These influential contacts gradually became the engine within Jimmy's burgeoning referral network.

Two months after Jimmy went from randomly shaking as many hands as possible to strategically building a tag team, wealthy entrepreneurs, prominent attorneys, corporate executives, and even a few reformed criminals were all sending him referrals every week. His reputation was growing fast. Now Jimmy needed to win a difficult case to prove his skills and begin making a public name for himself.

The chance came when one of Dan's clients was up against a DWI charge. The case was set for trial, but there was a problem. Dan was representing the star witness testifying in the Enron broadband trial. That trial was scheduled to take place at the same time as the DWI trial. There was no way Dan could take on both cases at the same time.

In a gutsy move, Jimmy went to Dan and told him not to worry. He had prepared the DWI case and was ready to try it *on his own*. He thought Dan's client was innocent, and he was going to prove it in front of a jury, despite the facts that said otherwise. Dan cautiously accepted the offer from his young protégé, so Jimmy went to court by himself for his first big jury trial. Before a packed courtroom, Jimmy argued as he had seen Dan argue back in that 2001 courtroom. The jury went into deliberation. Jimmy waited with his nervous client.

When the jury came back and took their seats, the foreman read the decision aloud, "Not guilty." Jimmy had just earned his first acquittal in a jury trial, and he had had his Bar Card for less than one year! Most of his law school classmates had not yet earned the right to file papers unsupervised, and he had just won his first *real* case. When Dan found out the jury's decision, he sent a mass e-mail to all the attorney's in his vast network proudly notifying them that his twenty-six-year-old protégé had just made a name for himself.

You may be wondering how smart Jimmy was to accept an offer of no salary but the opportunity to bring in his own clients. At the time, his law school classmates teased him for not securing a safe, stable salary. But all Jimmy needed was a chance to prove himself *and a high-performing tag team*. His first year is not over yet, but so far it appears he'll earn more money than *any* graduate at his competitive law school—and he'll also make some evening news shows.

Not bad for a C– graduate. All it took was plugging in and building a tag team that pulled him toward his dreams.

> **BOUNCED:** I can't make it because I don't have the right connections.
>
> **CASHED:** I can make it because the right connections are right under my nose!

TWO STEPS TOWARD BUILDING A TAG TEAM

In your own way, you are in the same real-world hit-or-miss position in which Jimmy began. You steer toward your future based on your dreams, the risks you're willing to take, what you learn along the way, and *the people you surround yourself with* to help you get there. You can try to travel the long road to your Future Picture alone, but when you're *alone* you're limited to your own individual talents, resilience, and abilities.

If you're brave enough to have a vision for your future greater than you alone can create, you will need a tag team who can help you get there. Your tag team enhances your knowledge, abilities, resilience, and talents and pushes you toward greater success *as if reaching your dreams were a team sport.* So where do you start?

Step 1: Find a Mentor

You begin to build your tag team by finding a mentor whom you trust, respect, and can count on. This mentor becomes the cornerstone of your tag team. Besides offering expertise and real-world contacts, your mentor must believe in you, possibly even more than you believe in yourself! Having a mentor who strongly believes in you makes a huge difference when life's not going your way. His unwavering belief inspires your belief. His wisdom guides your decisions. His contacts open doors you could not otherwise unlock. His previous success guides your future success.

Your mentor is your primary go-to resource when you have a big life question, simply need someone to listen, or feel overwhelmed. He keeps you focused on your priorities and usually has a gift for seeing the big picture when you see only frustration.

Your mentor stands by your side through the good and the bad. He doesn't give up on you when you fall on your face or when you land on your feet. Most likely, he has done both. He will not abandon you when your mouth outruns your abilities. But he will allow you to fail, so you can learn the tough lessons you need to move ahead. Your mentor knows that shaping your future helps shape his own legacy.

Mentors understand the power of a legacy, because they usually have had their own mentors. I know that all of my mentors have had their own mentors. In fact, one of my oldest mentors called me to share his excitement at finding a new mentor. I said, "You just got a new mentor? But you're sixty-four years old!" He said, "Yeah, but *he's* eighty!"

Many times, when a mentor and I are talking, she'll share word-for-word an insight she learned from *her mentor*. This inspires me, because it reminds me I'm part of something much bigger that I have a responsibility to continue. When you become a protégé, you extend this mentoring chain of unbroken knowledge.

The tremendous value that mentors bring to my life makes it difficult for me to listen to the ready-made excuses people our age use for not getting a mentor. Most people are smart enough to recognize the benefits of having a mentor, but they get stuck when it comes to actually going out and getting one. The twentysomethings I've interviewed who said they wanted a mentor but never got one usually hid behind three flimsy excuses:

1. I'm afraid of asking someone to be my mentor only to have her turn me down.
2. I'm too old to get a mentor.
3. I don't know how to get a mentor or what to do with one.

These excuses are all weak. Most people would be honored to be your mentor, and those who refuse do so because they're not right for you or where you want to go. From the mentors I have, and have had, I know that each mentoring relationship is different. But my own *all* started by my asking someone I respected for help and then growing the relationship at its natural pace. And learning that a mentor over sixty years old went out and got an even older mentor reminds me that *when you quit learning, you quit living*.

Put aside any excuses you have and go get your mentor! Your future deserves it. You may eventually have several mentors, each with her own area of expertise; but one thing is for sure: they will all surface after your first mentor has pushed you forward. To get your first mentor takes effort and a little bit of faith in yourself, but probably not as much as you think. In fact, if you *really* wanted to, I bet you could get a mentor in less than a month.

To win this bet, I developed the Thirty-Day Mentor Magnet. I know this approach works, because I've used it several times and so have many people I've taught. Now, all that stands between you and your mentor is thirty days and nine steps.

YOUR THIRTY-DAY MENTOR MAGNET CHECKLIST

1. **Decide why you need a mentor.** What is it that you want *so badly* that you believe a mentor can provide? Do you need someone to believe in you, someone to give you advice, or someone to

open doors? What can he help you do that you're having difficulty doing by yourself? The more specific your reasons for finding a mentor, the easier it will be to recognize and attract him.

2. **Create a list of people who can fill your needs.** Browse your cell phone directory and see if you have anyone's contact info who could be a potential mentor. Also consider people you may know casually, have worked for, or hung out with. Read your local paper and watch your local news to find out if someone in your town has been recognized for having what you need. If you went to college or grad school, ask your professors for suggestions. Keep your eyes and ears open *at all times* for your potential mentor. You'll see her once you start looking. I met one of my mentors backstage at a rock concert!

3. **Plug in beginning at the top.** Rank all the potential mentors you've identified in order of their fit for your needs. Starting with your number one choice, decide the best way to strategically plug in with each of them. Do you have his work phone number? How can you get it? Does he hang out at a social club? How can you get in? Is he a community or business leader? How can you get past his secretary? Keep improvising different ways to reach him. Get people in your existing network to help you, too. If that doesn't pay off, talk with people who might be clients of your potential mentor. This worked for Jimmy.

4. **Ask for ten.** Your potential mentor probably has lots of responsibilities, from work to family to volunteering. To grab her attention you must show up on her radar as a person of value, not a distraction. This means using every plug-in strategy from Chapter 5. Most people will give you ten minutes if you can just get to them and ask for it, *especially* if you call and ask every single day. Show her you value her time so much that you need only ten minutes.

5. **Show your value.** If your potential mentor is successful, rest assured that he had help getting there. Someone somewhere gave him a break, believed in him, or helped him out when he needed it most. Use this to your advantage by sharing what leads you to him. Be honest. The goal of your first meeting is to come across as *worth his time* by presenting yourself as ambitious, responsible, and full of potential. When you present yourself in this light he will want to mentor you, because you are a golden opportunity for him to build his legacy! Bring at least ten questions you want to ask, but don't worry if you get to only a few of them. If you don't feel that you're connecting well with your potential mentor, ask him for the names of two people he thinks might be able to better help you. Make sure you leave after ten minutes. Send him a handwritten thank-you card *the same day* you meet with him.

6. **Take a challenge.** If at the end of your initial meeting, you feel that you mesh well with this potential mentor, ask if you could meet with her again for ten minutes. If she accepts, ask what you can do between now and then to make the most of your next conversation. Ask if she can suggest any books you should read or actions you could take before you reconnect. This is *extremely* important. Accept the challenge and do it! Then you will have a perfect reason to call her for the next meeting. *You did what she said,* and now you're ready to talk about what you learned.

7. **Take it slowly.** When you next meet with your potential mentor, share what you learned from his challenge or assignment. If he asked you to read a book, tell him what you liked about it and what you didn't. If he asked you to volunteer, tell him what you saw. This is your chance to prove you're hungry, sharp, and worth his time. Not acting on his challenge shows him you don't deserve another meeting. After you share your experience and catch up, ask him if he would agree to be an infor-

mal adviser to you. Maybe he would agree to get together for twenty minutes a month? If he accepts, set some basic expectations for these regular meetings. If he declines to meet regularly, ask for leads to other people who might have what you need.

8. **Set expectations.** Being up-front with your expectations will reduce your new mentor's anxiety about committing to regularly meet with you. It will also decrease miscommunication later on. Basic expectations must include agreeing to confidentiality and how you will arrange meetings. My mentors and I tend to meet once a month. I usually set up the meeting through voice mail or e-mail. I bring the agenda and make sure we finish on time. Each meeting usually lasts about thirty minutes. Remember to turn off your cell phone, be on time, bring an agenda, ask questions, and listen.

9. **Create an adventure.** The more quality time you spend with your potential mentor, the sooner she will grow into your full-fledged mentor. Like any relationship, a mentoring relationship takes time and work, but the benefits are extraordinary. After my mentors and I have a good working relationship, I invite them to some type of community event or other activity where we can hang out in a more casual atmosphere. I have taken my mentors to charity fund-raisers, gone on a double date with them and their spouse, provided them a seat of honor at my birthday party, and traveled with them across the country. These out-of-the-office experiences provide great opportunities to get to know your mentor on a more personal level.

In the nine years that I've had mentors, they've made my life richer in so many ways. They've helped me grow my business and my spiritual understanding. They've connected me with my financial adviser, accountant, attorney, agent, and doctor.

They've been there to celebrate when I bought my first house. They've hosted me at their overseas homes and even introduced me to the president of the United States. They've helped me overcome the hurdles of going from a wide-eyed teen to a determined twentysomething.

Step 2: Assemble an All-Star Tag Team

Once you have your mentor, or are on your way to getting one, you're ready to start assembling the rest of your tag team. Creating your tag team is similar to recruiting for a professional sports team. You figure out where you're *strong* and where you're *weak*, and then seek tag team members who add to your strengths and compensate for your weaknesses.

The cornerstone of Jimmy's tag team is his mentor Dan Cogdell. Dan provides Jimmy with guidance, belief, and credibility, so what Jimmy needed to reach his Future Picture was client referrals. To get these referrals, Jimmy built an all-star tag team consisting of the influential people in his city: old-school millionaires, young high-tech executives, prominent attorneys who don't handle criminal defense—even a rap music producer. Each of these well-connected people brought his or her own skills, ideas, *and contacts* to Jimmy's quest. The sum of their networks explains Jimmy's rapid success and hints at what's possible *for you* when you create your own tag team.

In your case, the tag team you want to assemble may be to help you get into the grad school of your choice, earn a promotion at work, start your own business, or assist you in getting your first book published. Whatever Future Picture you want for yourself, building a tag team will make it easier to realize.

Twenty-seven-year-old Stephanie has seen a tag team turn her biggest insecurity into a point of strength and courage. Stephanie, like many twentysomethings, jumped into the work world right after graduating college. In the transition, she always had an excuse about why she shouldn't exercise or eat healthy. She assumed her metabolism would always keep her looking and feeling good. She was wrong.

About three years out of college she was so embarrassed to look in the mirror that she put her makeup on in the dark. She hated the way she now looked, but felt helpless about how to fix it. She more depressed she got about her body, the more junk food she ate, and the worse she felt. Then she went to the doctor for her annual checkup and learned that her cholesterol was off the charts. The doctor said she had to change her health choices or pretty soon she would be at risk of everything from a heart attach to diabetes. It was the wake-up call Stephanie needed.

The doctor suggested that Stephanie join a group of other women who were in a similar position. He said the camaraderie, emotional support, and accountability would help her get on the right path and stay there. Stephanie found a group like this in her community and began meeting twice a week. The sessions were part exercise, part cooking class, and part group therapy. At first Stephanie didn't want to open up, but when the group leader shared how she had lost over sixty pounds and kept it off Stephanie knew she was in the right place. It's been over a year since Stephanie joined her group, which she dubbed the Big Butts No-More, and she has lost over forty pounds! She says the secret to her success really isn't a secret: by surrounding herself with other people who cared about and supported her, there was no way she could fail.

Whether your vision for the future is starting a rock band, opening an art gallery, designing a new videogame, or losing forty pounds and keeping it off, your tag team will make reaching that vision easier and more likely. The seven positions you need to fill on your tag team should match your Future Picture and multiply your strengths.

YOUR SEVEN TAG-TEAM DRAFT PICKS

Niche Tag. Your Niche Tag has a skill, background, expertise, or talent that specifically fits one specialized area of your Future Picture. If you want to open an art gallery, this person would have owned an art gallery or have collected your type of art. If you want to design a new videogame, this person might be a software engineer or venture capitalist. If you want to lose forty pounds, this person should have lost the same or more. Your Niche Tag fits a specialized need that you must fill to reach your Future Picture.

List two people you know or know of who might serve as your Niche Tag:

Spiritual Tag. Your Spiritual Tag will help you find purpose, meaning, and significance in your life. This person might be of your preferred spiritual beliefs or someone you simply see as profoundly centered and peaceful. Your Spiritual Tag should challenge you to search for the deeper meaning in your life and help you experience a higher level of joy, love, and harmony.

List two people you know or know of who might serve as your Spiritual Tag:

Leadership Tag. Character is who you are and what you do when no one is looking. Leadership is the outgrowth of this character and determines if people will support you and follow your example. Leadership can be developed, especially with the guidance of someone who is a proven leader—your Leadership Tag. Experienced leaders can help you see the world through their eyes. They also can give you insight on how to act under pressure and stay true to your Future Picture. The better leader you become, the more of a difference you can make. Your Leadership Tag might be a grassroots community leader, former military officer, corporate executive, or someone else who you feel truly walks his talk.

List two people you know or know of who might serve as your Leadership Tag:

Financial Tag. Your Financial Tag should have her finances in order and be able to teach you how to do the same. She doesn't have to be a billionaire to be your Financial Tag, but she must have *personally* built her financial security. You will enhance her value by creating a solid relationship with a banker, accountant, and investment adviser—no matter how broke you think you are right now. In fact, the more in debt you find yourself, the more reason to get a Financial Tag! Whether you want to join the Peace Corps or become a neurosurgeon, finances will play a recurring role in your life. Get a Financial Tag on your side *early* and gain the peace of mind that comes with having a plan that puts what money you do have to use wisely.

List two people you know or know of who might serve as your Financial Tag:

Legal Tag. I never appreciated the importance of knowing a good attorney until I got caught in a legal dispute. Be sure to have a Legal Tag, even if that means only that you have the name and number of a credible attorney to call if someone crashes into your car and flees the scene, an old friend decides to sue you, or a roommate steals your stuff. Your Legal Tag may be a partner at a big firm or have a stand-alone office. The key is that any attorney you plan to use must have a winning track record. If you don't have hundreds of dollars to hire a lawyer as needed, become friends with a law school student or recent law school graduate who might be willing to help you for free or at a greatly reduced cost.

List two people you know or know of who might serve as your Legal Tag:

Wellness Tag. As you get older it becomes apparent—especially with the aches that seem to surface only in cold weather—that it's not simply how long you live but the quality of your life that matters. Your body is like any other biological system, it responds to what you do to it. Learning to care for your body *early* can help you avoid much of the irreparable damage that twentysomethings cause trying to work hard and play hard. Your Wellness Tag helps you stay healthy by keeping you focused on your physical and mental well-being. Your Wellness Tag does not have to be a doctor or licensed nutritionist, but he must live the healthy lifestyle that he advocates to you.

List two people you know or know of who might serve as your Wellness Tag:

Legacy Tag. The effect you have on future generations depends on the actions you take while you are alive. These actions create a ripple effect that extends beyond your own life and forms your legacy. You build your legacy by acting *now* to better the world, other people, and yourself. Your Legacy Tag should be someone who has established her legacy and wants to help you do the same. This person might have started a homeless shelter, begun a voter-registration campaign, or been an after-school tutor for troubled youth. Your Legacy Tag knows that by helping you build your legacy she expands her own!

List two people you know or know of who might serve as your Legacy Tag:

TAG—YOUR FUTURE'S IT!

When you feel you've secured your mentor and have most of your tag team positions filled, create a reason to bring your entire tag team together. Host a tag team appreciation dinner, sponsor a table at a charity event and invite them, or give each of your tag team members a place of honor at your next birthday party. When they see other quality people working hard to support you it will reinforce their own commitment!

INSTANT MESSAGE

► Your tag team consists of the people you can count on to pull you toward your Future Picture.

► Your mentor is the cornerstone of your tag team.

► When you build your tag team, you can achieve things far greater than your individual abilities.

BOUNCED: I can't make it because I don't have the right connections.

CASHED: I can make it because the right connections are right under my nose!

ONLINE: Watch Jimmy in action at
www.myrealitycheckbounced.com/book

7

WHAT'S PAST IS POWER

> What doesn't kill you makes you stronger when you choose to turn the experience into strength.

REALITY-CHECK MOMENT—
BASED ON MY PAST, I JUST DON'T
SEE HOW I CAN BE SUCCESSFUL.

So far we've talked a lot about where you want to go with your life and how to achieve your Future Picture. But it's also important to acknowledge and learn from where you've already been, so you can free yourself from any limitations of the past and reach boldly for what's possible.

We all have a past. This string of memories connects where we have been to where we are now. Ugly or pretty, everything you have experienced in the past has contributed to who you are now and what you are capable of achieving. In some cases, your memories can hold you back and cause you to be fearful and insecure. Left to run free in your imagination, your past can make you hesitant to dream big and live life to its fullest, sometimes because you have some painful memories you don't want to revisit. No matter how frightening events in your past may seem, it's all in your *past*—not your *future*. What you do from now on is your future.

Lindsay's past was so traumatic it almost did ruin her future. Until one fateful August moment, she was living a dream life. She graduated high school as captain of the cheerleading squad and number five academically in her class; she was voted by her classmates as most likely to succeed. To top it all off, she won Miss Teen America—dressed as a dancing broccoli for the talent competition!

In college, Lindsay had the time of her life. She lived with five of her closest friends. She was accepted into her dream sorority, Pi Phi. She earned a place in her college's exclusive Business Honors Program. The youngest child in a well-to-do family, Lindsay was a quick-witted beauty queen who had it all.

Until the jog. It was the day after her nineteenth birthday. To keep the "freshman fifteen" off, Lindsay left her apartment that afternoon to run at the city park down the street. Lindsay always wore headphones when she jogged. She loved to lose herself in her favorite music. This was a particularly happy day for her, because her mom and her boyfriend were in town to celebrate her birthday. They were all looking forward to a fun-filled celebratory dinner that evening.

It was August 14, 2000. As Lindsay neared the end of her jog, a stranger grabbed her from behind. He pressed a serrated knife against her throat and dragged her to a patch of over-grown grass in the middle of several dense trees. She pleaded for her life, but he didn't care. He ripped away her clothes and viciously stole her innocence.

When he was finished with his attack, he left her among the trees, alone and scared. She managed to find her torn clothes and get herself home. Her mom frantically called 911.

At the hospital the emergency room, staff took Lindsay through the standard rape protocol. As much as they helped clean her up, she still felt dirty. She felt violated. She felt empty. Most of all, she felt fear. She didn't want it to happen again, to her or anyone else.

A fighter at heart, Lindsay did not take long to recover physically. Then decided that nightmare in the park was not going to take her spirit. To prove it, she signed up for a marathon. Then she began regularly running with friends through the same park where her rape occurred. As long as she stayed busy, she could occasionally forget the pain.

However, the pain never went away for her boyfriend. It began to surface in their relationship. He became distant, reserved, and seemed to blame himself. Lindsay did not want to lose him. She thought opening up about the rape might rekindle their closeness. So she wrote him a letter detailing what happened that terrible afternoon in the park.

Sitting in her car as her boyfriend read the graphic letter, Lindsay was struck with a powerful realization—she herself was not healing. She was not moving forward. She was not getting better. The rapist was not in the car with her, yet he was still influencing her future.

The next day Lindsay and her boyfriend broke up. So she packed all her belongings and moved back home. She could not sleep that first night in her fluffy old bed. She could not even relax. She kept thinking how she had done nothing wrong, yet she felt so powerless and weak. She needed some sort of a guarantee that the painful violation would not happen again, but no such guarantee existed.

Lindsay and her family knew she couldn't go on this way. She had to recover the fragile sense of control that had been stripped from her. She started with the Internet.

Lindsay began to spend hours online reading about other women in her situation. Their stories helped her see that she was not alone. In fact, it's estimated that one in three women will be sexually assaulted during their lifetime. Reading first-person accounts of women living through this trauma gave Lindsay her first glimmer of hope: She too could survive.

FROM VICTIM TO SURVIVOR

Feeling secure became Lindsay's top priority. The security she needed arrived in the form of a cuddly but fierce German shepherd. Soon the two were inseparable. It was Lindsay's first baby step toward control, the first whisper of her moving on. It would slowly get easier.

Trauma in your past reenters your life in different ways. For Lindsay, she could not handle someone walking up behind her or physical contact. She knew this was unhealthy, so she began getting massages to regain comfort with human touch. This helped her learn trust again, hold someone's hand, sit comfortably at a crowded table.

After one semester at home with family and friends, Lindsay rebuilt the foundation of trust and control she needed. She saw it was okay to be scared and angry. She saw it was okay to cry at night. She was human.

Lindsay returned to college. By a stroke of incredible luck, the police apprehended the man they believed had assaulted Lindsay and several other young women. The district attorney called to tell Lindsay about the arrest. He told her the case was strong but not airtight. They needed a victim's testimony. All the other victims refused. Would Lindsay be willing to face her attacker?

On the witness stand, Lindsay's testimony was emotional, explicit, and powerful. The jury convicted him on all counts. The rapist was sentenced to life in prison without parole.

After sentencing, Lindsay learned she had the choice to speak to her rapist in open court before he went to prison. This is called a Victim Impact Statement. It's designed to help victims vent their emotions so they can begin to heal and move on from their painful experience. Lindsay took the stand once more. She looked her rapist square in the eye and got the closure rape victims rarely experience. She made every syllable count.

With the rape behind her, twenty-four-year-old Lindsay is now completing her second year of law school. She plans to become a prosecutor so she can help other victims regain their power. Here's how she's chosen to let this crime in her *past* influence her *future*:

After seeing the worst side of a human being, I got to see the best side of so many other people. Everyone has gut wrenching days when they get knocked down and shaken to their core. These sorts of things stay with you, no matter your age. I now see that if I hadn't confronted this trauma in my past it would have kept resurfacing in my life. By facing it head on, I trust myself once again.

This crime taught me to fight for what I want. I was put to the test. I lived. Now I know that whatever is thrown my way, I can get through it.

THE SHADOW YOU CAN'T OUTRUN

Lindsay was able to overcome an unimaginable trauma in her past by choosing to face it head on. By doing this, by confronting her demons, she was able to resume her life already in progress. Too many of us allow our past to deflate our courage, creativity, and spirit, when we have the choice to use what we've been through—*and survived*—to set us free.

Hidden within your past experiences are vivid examples of your character, choices, abilities, and attitude. You have memories of double-dares you still can't believe you accepted. You have memories of achievements that built your confidence and sucker punches that you want to forget. You also have memories of laugh-out-loud good times you want to bring back.

You may disagree, but taking a closer look at your past experiences reveals that everything in your life up to this point has happened for a reason—even if that reason was only to lead you to today.

The reasons behind your most difficult experiences may still seem painfully unclear. However, each of your setbacks, failures, and traumas can be turned into strength, which can propel you toward the Future Picture you most desire. This makes embracing the experiences of your past one of the best cheat sheets you have to improve yourself.

YOU BECOME WHAT YOU CHOOSE TO CARRY FROM YOUR PAST

The memories that make you feel most naked are the ones with the strongest emotional charge and unexplored meaning. These intense memories often involve embarrassing experiences, soured relationships, and personal failures. These emotionally powerful memories are the ones you must make peace with, learn from, and let go so you can *move on*.

Up to now, you may have chosen to hide from these tough memories rather than face them. Some of you have done this so well you are practically experts at hiding tough memories from yourself and others. Hiding from painful memories will not make them go away. In fact, the more you try to block out emotionally difficult memories, *the more you stay prisoner to them*. To put your toughest memories behind you for good, you must choose to make peace with them. When you have made peace with your toughest memories, you know they exist *but that they exist only in your past*.

PEACE BY PIECE

To come to terms with your past, you must be willing to confront it head-on. One way to do this is to get it all down on paper. When you chronologically chart the good and bad times in your past, you can see a roller-coaster ride of extreme highs and lows. These are your *defining moments*—the gut wrenching setbacks and inspiring breakthroughs that rocked you to your core. They are forever embedded in your memory, your view of the world, and your spirit.

The defining moments you can recall quickest and clearest are the ones most emotionally connected to who you are today. The vividness of these easy-to-relive memories makes them the ideal starting place to learn and grow.

Take a moment now to identify the defining moments in each decade of your life.

The three strongest memories you have up to age 10 (fifth grade) are

1. _____

2. _____

3. _____

The three strongest memories you have between ages 11 and 20 are

1. _____

2. _____

3. _____

The three strongest memories you have between ages 21 and 30 are

1. _____

2. _____

3. _____

The three strongest memories you have after age 30 are

1. _____

2. _____

3. _____

The emotionally powerful memories you just listed are your Decade Defining Moments (DDMs). These are the events in your past that, decade by decade, shaped who you are today. Some are good, some are bad, but all are unforgettable. Some helped you grow stronger immediately, whereas others took a while to recover from—but either way you carry a piece of them with you. For example, if you were teased as a kid for being overweight you might never get over it and miss how truly beautiful you are. Or you might have a memory of a boyfriend or girlfriend who broke your heart and as a result you never let anyone close again, which keeps you from ever realizing one snapshot within your Future Picture.

Once you choose to move beyond the emotional grip of your bad memories, you free yourself to focus *all* your energy on creating the future you want.

CUTTING THE ANCHORS OF YOUR PAST

Circle or star the three DDMs you believe have most negatively affected your life. These experiences clearly stand out in influence from the other significant memories you listed. These are the first three defining moments that you should learn from and let go, because making peace with them frees you from your heaviest anchors. You can then repeat this process with your other emotionally difficult memories until you totally free your future.

Whenever you recall your defining moments, good and

bad, you naturally replay them in your mind. In a sense, you bring these events from your past into your present. If you're a visual learner, you might see them in your mind as a movie. If you're a hands-on learner, you might physically reexperience them. If you're an audio learner, you might remember what the event sounded like. Whenever you replay your defining moments, you can tell if they make you feel sad, happy, alone, or inspired.

When a defining moment makes you feel pain, sadness, depression, or intense discomfort, it's an anchor that limits your progress and must be dealt with. To make peace with your toughest past experiences, you have two primary options: Either you can get professional help or you can choose to help yourself. If you want to get professional help, get it from someone experienced in this specific area. If you want to help yourself—like most twentysomethings—try following three steps to move beyond your toughest memories.

1. Add perspective.
2. Find the good within the bad.
3. Write a new ending.

To Add Perspective

Recognize that everything that happened in your past is forever locked in the past. No matter how real they seem in your imagination, your toughest memories are not happening now. Yes, whatever happened in your past did happen. Acknowledging this is important, but as important is acknowledging that it's over. The only thing happening right now is you.

To Find the Good within the Bad

Take out a piece of paper and make a list of three or four good things that eventually came out of each bad experience. Maybe you found out you were stronger than you thought, maybe you realized for the first time that people do love you, or maybe you were able to find a new opportunity. If you look hard enough you will be able to find specific, positive things that came out of even your most difficult situation. This will help you see that no matter how tough life gets, you still leave every situation in some way better than when you began.

To Write a New Ending

Writing a new ending to your toughest memories does not change what happened. However, it signals to your brain that your bad memories are not in control of your future or how you see the world. When you write a new ending to your toughest memories, your brain recognizes you are living in the present, not the past. Rewriting your toughest memories also helps highlight what you have learned from them.

On a new piece of paper, describe what happened during your three toughest defining moments—for example, your parents getting divorced, a grandparent dying, losing your job, or having your heart broken. Skip a few lines and then write a more fulfilling, inspiring, and happy ending to those memories. Show on paper that by writing a new ending you are no longer emotionally limited by what you did not know or could not know at that time. Prove to yourself in writing what you have learned since then. You are now stronger and wiser. You are now in control of your future. And you have the paper to prove it!

Your toughest memories, as horrible as they may seem, still led to positive outcomes—probably *many* positive outcomes. Sometimes you just have to bravely look beyond your hurt to find them. Once you have made peace with the toughest parts of your past, you are free to learn from them, let go of them, and get a move on. Your past is over. *You are the present.*

You will know you have freed yourself to boldly reach for your future when you can honestly say, "It was important that

_____ happened, because it helped me be as loving, resilient, and passionate as I am today." With this statement, you tell yourself you have the freedom to focus on the present, so you can create the future you want.

> **BOUNCED:** My past determines my future.
>
> **CASHED:** I can put my past to work to create the future I want.

POP QUIZ: ARE YOU WISE BEYOND YOUR YEARS?

Have you ever met someone younger than you who seemed impossibly wise for his age? What gave him such street smarts so early in life? Did he overcome some daunting challenge? Did his education or career take him around the world? Did he get married young? Did he finish a marathon? Did he leave home early?

My interviews with peers who seemed wiser than their age taught me that they are no smarter than you or I. They just did a better job of turning their past experiences—good and bad—into practical knowledge. They paid attention to their mistakes so they would not repeat them, and they paid attention to their successes so they could repeat them. When you pay attention to your past you have to pay only once.

For every minute you spend learning from your past, you save hours of future frustration.

Start getting wise beyond your age by answering these questions:

1. What is the biggest lesson you've had to learn the hard way?
2. What constructive criticism do you get most from people you respect and trust?
3. What have you repeatedly done that keeps you from success?

4. What do you do that successfully keeps you on track during difficult times?
5. What do people say are your two biggest strengths, skills, or talents?
6. What has been your greatest achievement so far?

Your answers to questions 1–3 help you see strategies and actions that *have not* worked for you. Knowing this tells you to not repeat them. If it didn't work the first twenty-five times, it's time to try something new! Possible examples in your past: not being willing to meet new people, overcommitting so you set yourself up for failure, sabotaging relationships by not being trustworthy, running up crazy credit-card bills and then not paying.

Your answers to questions 4–6 help you see what strengths *you can rely on* in your relentless push toward your Future Picture. These strengths will help you when you're part of a team and when you're forced to stand alone. Keep building on your strengths, and they can more than compensate for your weaknesses. Do what works! Possible examples in your past: working well on tight deadlines, resolving conflicts among other people, being a good friend, sticking to an exercise routine and a budget.

Answering these six questions in your own words gives you a good idea of *why* you are where you are. Pay attention to your weaknesses, and you'll see where to improve. Pay attention to your strengths, and you'll see where to create more success in your future. The key is to pay attention *now* so you, too, have to pay only once!

TIE UP LOOSE ENDS OR FIND YOURSELF IN KNOTS

The final step toward putting your past behind so you can reach for what's possible is tying up your loose ends. Loose ends are the unresolved relationships that keep you from sleeping worry free at night.

Skeletons are hard to keep buried because they always have a bone to pick.

You have a loose end, if there's someone you don't want to see at the grocery store or movie theater. You have a loose end, if there's someone you don't want to run into on a first date or at work. You have a loose end, if there's someone you don't want to sit next to at a holiday dinner. Loose ends are distracting and have an amazing way of biting you in the butt at the worst times.

When loose ends are lurking in the back of your mind, they take your focus off doing what it takes to succeed. Loose ends bring you back to a place where you don't want or need to go. Loose ends must be tied up so they cannot run free to steal your confidence and concentration. Tying up loose ends allows you to totally focus on doing what you need to do to get where you want to go.

For example, if you borrowed money from someone and never paid her back, you have to always worry about running into her at the wrong time, like when you're already late for a date or out shopping with your mom. Instead of facing these embarrassing scenarios, have the courage to call your lender up and agree to repay her a little bit every week until you are square. You'll be amazed how a little effort on your part can salvage broken relationships and let you walk once again with your head held high.

How to Tie Up Your Loose Ends

1. **Identify the five people with whom you have the most unresolved issues.** These could be past relationships, employers, business partners, friends, family, or co-workers. These are people you avoid talking with and running into.

2. **Contact each of these five loose ends.** Invite each separately to a coffee shop or some other nonthreatening, nonalcohol environment. Tell each one that you want to apologize for allowing things to get crossways between you. Even if she was the one who hurt you, tell her you want to move on. Some may doubt your intentions, but tell them that you sincerely feel its time to clear the air. Ask those who agree to meet to write down any ways they think you wronged them, and you do the same. Tell them to bring this list to your get-together.

3. **Show up on time and thank each for being forgiving enough to meet with you.** Tell each person that you want to apologize for whatever you did that hurt him (even if you don't completely agree with his view of the situation). Be an adult here; finger pointing only tears people apart. Remember, your experience may be—and most likely is—totally different from his. Listen to each issue each of them raise and try to see it from their perspectives. Don't interrupt them when they are sharing. Seek to understand why they harbor bad feelings toward you. Apologize for each thing they think you did to wrong them. If you're nervous about apologizing, go ahead and practice in a mirror before each meeting.

4. **At the end of the conversation, thank each once again for talking with you.** It was a big show of faith in your character. Plus, she's helping you to move toward your dreams by tying up loose ends in your past. The next day, send her a handwritten card thanking her for reconnecting. You can then decide whether or not to stay in touch.

After you tie up your first loose end, you'll want to resolve them all. This is hard to explain until you have done it; but once you do, you'll know what I mean. I learned so much about myself by tying up my loose ends. Most of all, I think this process helped me become a more understanding and patient friend.

I have one of my mentors to thank for this advice and my freedom from loose ends. Three years ago, he made me tie up all my loose ends. He told me that the only way he would continue mentoring me was if I agreed to do this. I tried to get out of this challenge, but my mentor was not accepting excuses. I finally gave in and invited one of my former friends for coffee and a sincere apology.

This meeting was *very* uncomfortable. In fact, my former friend and I had been avoiding each other for the better part of two years! At first, I didn't really know what to say, so I took my mentor's advice, and it proved to be one of the most liberating risks I've ever taken. I asked my former friend to bring a written list of what he felt I did to wrong him. His list was more like an essay; he had fifteen or twenty items written down! I then asked him to go line by line down the list. As he shared with me each thing that was bothering him, I tried to see it through his perspective. Then I swallowed my pride and apologized for each thing. It was not easy, but tying up this loose end was absolutely worth it.

By the end of his list, it was clear to both of us that every issue he brought up hinged on one thing: He felt that I had abandoned him at his most difficult time. He was right. When he needed me the most, I was not there. I was too concerned about how his crisis would affect my own reputation. He eventually got through that mess, but we never reconnected.

That afternoon, my old friend and I talked through all our unresolved issues. We agreed that we each had a very different interpretation of what led us apart. This agreement evaporated the tension between us. He hadn't understood my motives, and I hadn't understood the extent of his situation. Not talking only made it worse.

I felt so much better after tying up this first loose end that I immediately set up meetings with all my other ones. To my surprise, they all agreed to meet with me. At the end of my mentor's challenge to tie up my loose ends, I got three old friends back. I also reconnected with a former mentor. Most freeing, I no longer worry about running into an ex-girlfriend who I thought held a grudge against me. Turns out, she just wanted to know if we could be friends.

Tying up my loose ends showed me how two people can leave one past experience with two totally different perspectives. This difference in perspectives can lead to two totally different emotional reactions. This is especially true when other unspoken issues lie under the surface. Making the effort to tie up my loose ends showed me that, with a little effort, most people are forgiving. I also learned how great it feels to go anywhere and not worry about running into someone you don't want to see!

TURN YOUR PAST INTO A BRIGHTER FUTURE

Twenty-six-year-old Randy will never forget the day his high school guidance counselor told him he wasn't college material. She said with his grades and attitude he should focus on getting a job and be happy with whatever he got, because it was the best he could hope for. Rather than heed her advice, he transferred to an alternative high school, earned his diploma, and then enrolled in a local community college.

Five years and three colleges later, Randy—the hardheaded kid who was told he wasn't college material—graduated college *on the dean's list*. He is now a twenty-six-year-old manager of a health-care clinic. Instead of sitting around resenting his high school counselor's shortsighted advice, he has turned his past into something positive. Now he makes a point of hiring young people who can't get a job because of their lackluster grades. He realizes that if you give people like him a chance they just might surprise you!

Give your future a chance by facing your past—and choosing to turn it into a strength. After all, your past made you who you are, and it gives you the power to *choose* who you are determined to become.

INSTANT MESSAGE

► Don't run from your past. Use it to fuel your future.

► Once you add perspective to your past, you can learn its lessons.

► Tie up your loose ends, and you free your future.

BOUNCED: My past determines my future.

CASHED: I can put my past to work to create the future I want.

ONLINE: Watch Lindsay share about dealing with her past at **www.myrealitycheckbounced.com/book**

8

CHECK YOUR EXCUSES AT THE DOOR

> You can create excuses or you can create solutions, but you can't create both at the same time.

REALITY-CHECK MOMENT:
BUT LIFE'S JUST NOT FAIR!

At some point in your quest to triumph in the real world, you will hit a roadblock (or twelve). Roommates will steal from you. Job interviews will go poorly. Your girlfriend will dump you. Your boyfriend will get needy. A close friend will die. And you'll come to the sobering conclusion that maybe you're not good enough, old enough, smart enough, attractive enough, or strong enough to live the life you dream about. The real question is: How will you handle these setbacks and the insecurities they create? Will you quit on your dreams? Will you smother your opportunities with excuses? Will you point fingers and blame other people for your situation?

Or will you show the world what you're really made of, like Sean? Sean is a twenty-three-year-old who suffers from osteogenesis imperfecta (OI), a rare brittle-bone disease. When he was born, the doctors told his parents he would not live through the night. They were wrong. Sean is alive and determined to be heard. Or, as he often jokes, he's alive, and all those doctors are dead. It helps to have a sense of irony know-ing that every time you laugh you risk breaking a rib or collar bone.

Four years ago I met Sean for the first time. Like the doc-tors surrounding him at his birth, I could see he was different. It was hard to miss; he was full grown at three feet tall.

He explained to me that every morning when he wakes up, he faces a decision few of us can imagine: Find out what abil-ities his body offers that day or stay in bed. It would be hard to criticize him if he chose to play it safe by staying in bed. His disorder is a legitimate medical condition. Who could blame him for not taking risks when his bones are so fragile they could break when he shakes hands?

Sean sees his situation differently:

The turning point in my life was fourth grade. It was Halloween. The one day a year when I don't stick out in a crowd. On Halloween, everyone looks different.

I was out of my wheelchair, playing on my living room floor, scooting around on my stomach. I had on my Halloween costume and was so excited to show it off to my friends at school. In my excitement, I accidentally caught my left leg on the corner of the doorway, and I heard the bone snap.

My mom heard me yelling and raced down the stairs to reach me. My heart was pumping so fast my breath could not catch up. I knew weeks of staying immobilized in one position lay ahead.

I kept thinking, "Why me? What did I ever do to deserve this pain?"

Running her fingers through my damp hair, Mom calmly looked into my eyes. She tried to take my mind off the throbbing pain, but it wasn't working. So she softly asked, "Sweetheart, is this [the disease] going to be a blessing or a burden?" At that moment, I felt a peace and clarity that fifteen years later still gives me chills. Until that question, all I could think about was the pain and suffering of my condition.

Up to that point, I thought about being carried between classes at my elementary school, because it was not wheelchair accessible. I thought about people staring at me everywhere I went. I thought about all the things I couldn't do, not all the things I could.

Lying in my mom's safe arms, I decided my imperfect bones might be a blessing after all. If I could live through this pain, I could probably help other people do the same.

I went through elementary school, middle school, and high school with a new attitude. At the end of my junior year in high school, I decided to run for student council president. It was one of the few activities my bones allowed. The people with regular bones could play football, basketball, or run track. I had student council.

I put all my energy into winning that campaign. I worked ten times harder than my competition. I was sure I was going to win! I waited with my friends for the big news of my victory. Then my heart sank. I learned that I had lost to a popular cheerleader. I felt angry and jealous.

Her bones worked fine, she didn't even campaign. Why did she have to steal the one thing I could do? I was ready to quit school altogether, but then I remembered my mom's Halloween question. Was this going to be a blessing or a burden? At this lowest teenage point, recalling my mom's question helped me get back in control of my attitude.

HIS BIGGEST BREAK OF ALL

I decided I was not going to let one defeat ruin my life. Two weeks later, I was invited to Boys State, a statewide young leader's conference with over a thousand participants. At this *conference, I once again ran for office, but this time I was elected governor—the highest position. It was then that I learned I had received a surprise invitation to meet President Clinton!*

Two years later, he offered me an internship at the White House. Sounds too good to be true I know, but it's not. If I had given up on myself after losing my high school student council race, I would never have taken the risks that led to me meeting the president. I would have missed out on an opportunity that completely changed what I thought I could do with my life.

By the time I graduated high school, I had had over two hundred "breaks." I wanted to attend college, but there was no way I could physically go alone. So my dad agreed to be my full-time assistant at college, while my mom became the sole financial supporter of our family. This put us in a tough financial position, but my parents wanted me to have the best education possible. They are that selfless.

During high school, I had done some public speaking in my community about living with a disability. But during my freshman year of college all kinds of groups started asking me to speak at their events. They wanted me to talk about my experience growing up but not giving up.

Watching the faces in the audiences go from laughing to crying to thinking, it struck me that every one of us has our own breaks in life. These are times when life just doesn't seem fair. My message was the same at each speech: Life is full of pain. Suffering is optional. Excuses only extend your suffering.

After graduating college, I realized that inspiring people through speaking and writing was my life purpose. Now I'm in my mid-twenties and have built a successful career spreading my message to audiences around the world. I've even gone back to school to earn my Ph.D., so I can take my teaching to another level. Helping people deal with the breaks in their lives is the best job in the world.

And who knew that my mom was right all along? My imperfect body is the perfect vessel for my message. Yes, adults still gawk. My bones still break—but not my spirit. Life is full of pain. Suffering is optional. Excuses only extend the suffering."

In 2001, Sean proved how strongly he lives his message. That year, he released his first bodybuilding video, co-hosted with the former Miss Fitness USA. *Yes, you read that right.* The guy whose bones can break when you shake his hand has a video on how to get a six-pack and rippling muscles *like him.* That's Sean. His brittle bones might be a burden, but he has chosen to make them a blessing.

CRIERS VS. TRIERS

By this point in life, you know that life is not always fair. But like Sean, *you get to choose how to handle the times when life throws you a curve.* You can make excuses, point fingers, blame your situation on everything and everybody but yourself. Or you can throw yourself at life's twists and turns knowing that, win or lose, you'll come out stronger and feeling more alive.

In fact, every setback you survive and mistake you make teaches you valuable lessons that prepare you for greater success with the next challenge you face. When you make excuses, you deny yourself this golden learning opportunity and instead set yourself up for repeated disappointment. Every hurdle you choose to confront head-on rather than hide from with excuses moves you closer to what you most want.

I first learned life was not fair at age nine, when my parents divorced. My mom moved my brother and me to a small town far from our old home. I seemed so different from the other kids and didn't really fit in. Then to add insult to injury, my grandmother passed away unexpectedly. I really looked up to her. Losing her was like losing a big hug. When I finally started high school, I was a towering four foot ten—in shoes—and had a girly voice. One of my teachers always called me "chicken legs." Later I got rejected from twelve colleges, had to bus tables while my friends went on summer vacation, and even published my first book myself—because I didn't know how else to get its message out.

Today I understand how these challenges, sucker punches, setbacks, and disappointments prepared me for the dream I now live. Starting over in a small town taught me what it was like to not fit in and how to make it work. Being short in high school taught me how to use my wit to make up for my height. Learning about death early helped me appreciate my own life. Doing manual labor—washing dishes and mowing yards— taught me that I preferred to work smarter not harder. Getting rejected from so many colleges landed me at the college where I met a mentor who changed my life. Publishing my first book myself launched me into an entrepreneurial world of fascinating people and adventures that I cherish. Yes, life is not fair— and thank goodness for that—because when we recognize it's not fair we can choose to make it work *anyway*. This *choice* to succeed, no matter the curve balls and sucker punches, is what determines how far you go.

How you choose to deal with life not being fair directs the course of your life. Some people use it as a handy excuse to play the blame game. They blame everything and everyone *but themselves* for their misfortunes and unhappiness. These finger-pointers force themselves to stay weak, uninspired, and spin their wheels. They become bogged down in their own excuses and can become old and bitter, unless they realize they have the power to make another, wiser choice about how to deal with life being unfair.

Christina is a perfect example of someone who has stalled out because her excuses won't let her move forward. Her dad said he'd pay for her college and then backed out leaving her with mountains of debt. Her younger brother got arrested for drugs, and she had to bail him out, literally. Her mom is bipolar and goes from acting like a mom to acting like a stranger.

Christina bitterly blames her dad for not keeping his word and forcing her to work two jobs during college. She blames herself for her brother's decision to hang out with thugs. She blames her mom for not being there when she needed her most. Her family, she says, is so messed up that it has consumed her life. She blames them for standing in the way of her dreams. It's true she's had some terrible luck, but will anything positive ever come from her choice to be so resentful and act as if she has no control over her life?

TRYING TO WIN BY QUITTING AT HALFTIME

Other twentysomethings realize life's not fair, and rather than make the effort to create excuses they react by simply refusing to try. They may even have the audacity to tell themselves, "If I don't really try, then I never really fail." What a load of junk! *The only way you can fail in life is by not acting on your dreams.* When you don't pursue your dreams with all you've got, you sabotage your chance to live a life of meaning—no matter how you try to put a positive spin on it.

Twenty-six-year-old Zack is one of those "I'm successful because I've never failed" people. He brags about his big plans for the future, and how he's going to be rich, famous, respected, and admired. He acts very egotistical and boastful about where he's headed, but it's all a facade. It's the only way he knows how to put a positive spin on being unemployed, sleeping in his childhood bedroom, and having a curfew—at age twenty-six! Anyone who hangs out with him for more than ten minutes sees through his act and into how empty he actually feels. Yet, it's been four years since he graduated college and he has taken zero steps toward living his big talk. At this rate he'll be thirty and still pretending he's a success, even though he sleeps in a room with posters of his teen idols on the wall! Choosing not to try is as damaging to your future as smothering yourself in excuses because, either way, you give up control of your life, your happiness, and your dreams.

Are you like Zack or Christina? Or are you someone who genuinely feels a pull to have your life mean something? Someone who realizes life may not be fair, but you are determined to make it work *anyway*. It's this attitude of personal responsibility and resilience that will keep you pushing forward when all appears lost. Release your excuses and take control of how you handle everything life throws your way. It's time for you to kick your own "but . . ."!

BOUNCED: I would like to succeed, but . . .
CASHED: I will succeed—no ifs, ands, or buts about it.

When you refuse to make excuses, you put yourself at an instant advantage. You position yourself to *immediately* learn from setbacks, challenges, missed opportunities, and disappointments. These seemingly expensive real-life lessons become bargains because they keep you from repeating costly mistakes and help you get wiser faster to what works in the real world.

The opposite happens when you make excuses. The moment you blame anyone or anything for your predicament, you tell your brain it is okay to *stop* trying to solve your problem. You are setting yourself up to repeat the same mistakes again and again and again.

At the same time, while hiding behind excuses makes it harder for you to learn important lessons, it also makes it more difficult for other people to step up and help you when you need it most. Why? When you make excuses, you make it difficult for other people to . . .

1. **Trust you**: your excuses show that *your word is not your bond.*
2. **Help you**: your excuses show that *you don't want to help yourself.*
3. **Teach you**: your excuses show that *you are not hungry to learn.*

Throw away your excuses, and your mind will begin to see new solutions to old problems. Your character will attract the people you need on your tag team. Your confidence will grow with each challenge you are able to conquer. Throw away your excuses, and you can grab on to something solid: your future!

YOUR EXCUSES—EXPOSED

To help you get rid of your excuses so you can get on with your life as quickly as possible, you need to identify your biggest excuses and what to do about each one. Some of these excuses I've covered in earlier chapters: the "I don't have any connections" excuse, the "my past keeps holding me back" excuse, and the "I don't know what I want to be when I grow up" excuse. I hope, we can start putting those to bed—or at least give them a nap!

I've compiled a list of other classic excuses that most keep our generation from reaching our goals. Before I share them with you, I challenge you to write the three excuses you rely on most often. If three excuses don't immediately come to mind, think of what you said the last time you tried to talk your way out of trouble, the primary reasons you believe you won't reach your biggest goals, or the three barriers that have consistently held you back.

- **Excuse 1:** _____
- **Excuse 2:** _____
- **Excuse 3:** _____

I know that most of you won't write your three biggest excuses. But let's pretend you did. The excuses you would have written represent deep fears that you may or may not want to address. You'll learn more about these in Chapter 9. For the moment, just recognize that the excuses *you choose to use* limit your life, progress, and experiences.

So why do you continue to use them? Over time, your excuses feel safe, comfortable, and predictable—like a virtual security blanket. They insulate you from the unpredictable harsh realities of a world that doesn't always go your way. This virtual security blanket *tricks you* into thinking a situation or setback isn't your fault, responsibility, or problem. Unfortunately, this security blanket *is imaginary*. In the real world, the decisions you make and the path you take are *your choice*—and your choice alone. Excuses only limit your power to choose where you go from here.

To get somewhere more fulfilling than where you are now, you will have to let go of the excuses that hold you back. Here's the terrific news: You chose to create your excuses, so you can choose to get rid of them.

Start by admitting your top three excuses—or the ones

closest to them. Read what the excuse says about you and what you must do to get it out of your life. Once you have taken these steps, you will be primed to handle whatever twists and turns invariably come your way.

SEVEN EXCUSES TO ELIMINATE TODAY

1. The Age Excuse

When you hide behind your age, your time on earth quickly becomes more than just a number. You show that you attack an unhealthy expectation of opportunity, achievement, progress, or status to that one number. Maybe you are telling yourself that you should be more successful? Maybe you are telling yourself that success is only possible for older people? Maybe you are telling yourself that you're the wrong age for your ambitions? Whatever your age hang up, you must get rid of it, if you want to live your dreams at *any* age. Give up trying to change the past. Give up trying to predict the future. Blow out your birthday candles, roll up your sleeves, and put yourself on a path to live like you mean it!

Typical Defeatist Declaration: No one will want to marry me—I'm too old.

From the X-Cuse Files

Julie turned thirty-six recently. It was a sad day for her because she thinks she is now officially too old to get married and raise a family. As a result she's started dating loads of losers—in a twisted way of creating a self-fulfilling prophecy—and her spirit is only getting lower. As long as she thinks her age determines her marriage options, she won't have the choice to build the family she's always wanted.

Moving Beyond the Age Excuse

Step 1: Recognize that there is no right age to succeed, only *right now*. The key is *don't use your age as an excuse* to keep from trying. Focus on succeeding in the present.

Step 2: Interview two people you think are successful, who also began their journey or reached their success at your current age. Find out how they used their age to their advantage. See what they can share with you to help you do the same.

Step 3: Write down three reasons why your age makes you uniquely suited for the success you desire. Carry this list in your wallet or purse.

Step 4: Take a baby step past your age insecurity by refusing to use your age as an excuse for two weeks. Ask a friend whom you trust to point out whenever you use your age as an excuse. When you catch yourself doing this, immediately tell yourself two reasons why your age is actually an advantage. Notice how you feel about your age at the end of the two weeks.

Step 5: Take a big leap past your age excuse by putting yourself in the path of success *now*. Apply for three jobs that fit what you want. Volunteer for a charity that stretches you toward your vision of success. If you're like Julie, don't accept that age has anything to do with finding Mr. Right. Instead, raise your standards and see what kind of potential spouse *that* attracts!

2. The Education (or Lack of) Excuse

Depending on your Future Picture, formal education may be a prerequisite for living your dream. If you want to be a plastic surgeon, for example, you need a medical degree. For other paths, however—such as becoming a best-selling author, award-winning graphic designer, or starting your own school-reform movement—what you need more than a degree is a willingness to learn, work hard, and ask for help so you can pave your own path. Usually a lack of education doesn't ultimately keep people from their dreams, but rather a lack of desire *to do what it takes* to make that path.

Typical Defeatist Declaration: I don't have the right degree to do what I really want.

From the X-Cuse Files:

Gladys knows how to style hair. She went to beauty school and graduated at the top of her class. For the last nine years, she's built a loyal following of clients styling hair at a small salon on the outskirts of a big city. As happy as Gladys appears to her clients, she dreams about one day opening up her own hair salon. It's a dream she'd had for years. But Gladys won't give her dream a chance because she thinks that without a college degree she'll never be able to get the loan she needs to start her own salon.

Moving Beyond the Education (or Lack of) Excuse

Step 1: Accept it's not how smart you are, *it's what you do with what you have!* You don't have to have straight A's to be president of the United States, hold two Ph.D.s to be a billionaire, or graduate from an Ivy League college to be a successful trial lawyer. You just have to *use what you've got* to the best of your abilities.

Step 2: Assess your intellectual strengths to see if there are areas in which you need to improve. If so, get help. No one has to know except you and the person helping you. If your insecurity runs deeper, build your confidence through small successes.

Step 3: If you do feel that there is just no way you can pursue your dream without a certain degree, then rearrange your calendar and get one. Your commitment to attending night school, weekend classes, or going through specialized training will only reinforce your enthusiasm for where you are going.

Step 4: Help others build their smarts and you'll improve your own. Mentor a sixth grader in reading. Tutor a third grader in math. Once a week, practice English with someone who needs the help. So many people can benefit from your sharing your knowledge. Doing this will also make you feel great!

Step 5: Push beyond your intelligence comfort zone. Ask to lead a big project at work, read a thick book full of long words, or write a business plan for your great idea.

3. The Family Excuse

The vision of a close-knit, loving family that supports you as you spread your wings is a universal ideal. But for many twenty-somethings getting along with family is not always that easy and not just during the holidays. In your world, you might have a parent, relative, sibling, or spouse that doesn't agree with you, your friends, your decisions, or your dreams. He may say that he loves you, but it sure doesn't feel like it.

There comes a time in your life when you must make the decision whether you are going to live to make your family happy or live to make yourself happy. It's not a simple choice, but it's a pivotal one. If you go against your family's wishes, there will be consequences, but following your heart does give you the chance to live with meaning and purpose. If you choose to play it safe and follow your family's advice, give yourself some time to see if that path ends up feeling right.

Typical Defeatist Declaration: My family doesn't believe in me.

From the X-Cuse Files:

Blane knows what it feels like to go against your family's wishes. He had a great relationship with his family until, at age twenty-three, he realized he was gay. This decision was more than his family could handle. When he told his mom she cried and cried. His father told him he was ashamed and to never speak to him again. As far as his parents were concerned, Blane was no longer their son—unless he changed his ways. For a long time he used his family's rejection as an excuse to not pursue his dream of becoming a chiropractor. He thought if his family didn't want him, neither would any reputable chiropractic school. Blane finally came to his senses and is now finishing his first year at chiropractic school.

Moving Beyond the Family Excuse

Step 1: Write down what your family does that keeps you from your dreams. Do they not believe in you? Do they put you down? Do they not offer their help? Then answer: Do you think they're doing this to protect you or are they trying to sabotage your success?

Step 2: Ask your family, or the challenging family member, to talk with you in private. Tell her you want to talk about your future, and that you value her opinion *so much* you want her advice. Set aside twenty minutes of undisturbed time. Turn off your cell phone, go to a neutral place, and talk with her face to face.

Step 3: Tell the family member that you are at an important crossroad. You have some big decisions to make. Then explain your options, and ask what she would do in your situation and why. Make the effort to listen to her, so she will make the effort to listen to you. Then reverse this role-play situation and tell her what you would say if you were in *her shoes*. Finally, tell her what decision you are planning to make and ask if she understands why you feel hurt by the things she's previously said or done.

Step 4: After you've each shared your perspective and motivations, tell her why your decision is so important to you. Let her see your passion for living your dream. Ask her if she is willing to try being supportive. Thank her for caring enough about you to consider your view.

Step 5: Take a few days to think about her comments. Then make your decision. Make your decision out of purpose and wisdom, not pride or stubbornness. Be clear on how you will measure your progress. Be open to trying different paths if this one doesn't bring you the joy you want.

Step 5.5: Keep your parents involved throughout your journey. Choose a way to regularly communicate with them that is effective and easily maintained. This might be a weekly phone call or e-mail. Lack of communication leads to lack of trust, which leads to hurt feelings. Treat your family as you want them to treat you—and eventually they will!

4. The Location Excuse

Wherever you live—be it rural Kansas or East L.A.—I'm sure if you look hard enough you can find a way to use your ZIP code as an excuse for why you should give up on your dreams. Maybe the people in your town are small-minded, maybe there are no colleges nearby, maybe your neighborhood is unsafe, maybe everyone looks and acts the same way, or maybe you just see no path from where you are to where you want go. The point: We can all find something wrong with where we live.

Typical Defeatist Declaration: I wasn't born on the right side of the tracks, so no one will ever take me seriously.

From the X-Cuse Files:

D'anica has seen what survival of the fittest is all about. She lives in a rough neighborhood on the outskirts of a decaying Rust Belt city. She's seen a friend of hers shot. She's seen family members arrested. She's seen what a neighborhood looks like when there are no jobs. She's seen way too much for someone barely twenty, and she's seen enough to believe there is no way out. The only path she sees is to not be a snitch, build a reputation for not backing down, and try to live as long as she can.

Moving Beyond the Location Excuse

Step 1: Identify two ways to turn wherever you live into an advantage to you reaching your Future Picture. Maybe you live in a tough neighborhood, so you have street smarts. Maybe you live in a small town, so you know how to use gossip to your benefit. Maybe you grew up in the suburbs, so you are good at handling peer pressure. Get clear on the strengths you have because of where you live or where you grew up.

Step 2: Go online and explore your options. If you don't have a computer, go to your local library, workforce development center, or borrow a friend's. The Internet shatters the ZIP code barrier to information!

Step 3: Take a hands-on approach. If you want to become an actor in L.A., drive, take a bus, or fly to L.A. Hang out and see if you like the city. If you want to start your own business, find someone who lives near you and owns his own business. Take him to lunch and learn how he did it. If you want to go to grad school, visit as many as you can. Sit in on classes and buy a bumper sticker.

Step 4: Interview two people who have made the jump from your geographic location to where you want to go. Most organizations, from entrepreneur associations to colleges and employers, will connect you with people from your geographic location. These people will know what you need to learn so you can make the jump toward your dreams.

Step 5: Start opening doors from where you are now. Enroll in a community education program, apply for a loan to start your business, ask successful people for help. Use your location as a geographic advantage, and you will find the high ground!

5. The Money Excuse

Money—the word alone triggers many emotions. Many people use having no money as an excuse not to chase their dreams. In doing so, they're basically saying to the world, "I don't want to try that hard to succeed." Others are fearful of having to take responsibility once they make money or they fear losing what they already have. Either way, if left unchallenged, excuses about money may very well bankrupt your spirit.

Typical Defeatist Declaration: I don't have enough money to succeed.

From the X-Cuse Files:

Max wants to travel the world. The thought of visiting exotic lands and meeting new people gets his heart beating. He's convinced that being a steward of humankind is his purpose in life. His only hurdle: He can't seem to save enough money to make the trip. Every time he gets close, he spends his savings, and he's broke again. In the five years he's talked about seeing the world, the only progress he's made is coming up with new excuses of why he can't afford to go.

Moving Beyond the Money Excuse

Step 1: Get the facts on your financial situation. Add up how much money you make each month and subtract from that how much you spend each month. If you end up with a negative number, it's *urgent* for your financial health (and peace of mind) that you either start spending less or earning more—pretty simple if you think about it.

Step 2: Reduce your credit-card debt. Open those thick monthly statements and find out the total amount you owe. Pay *at least* the minimum on each of them, and pick the one with the highest interest rate to pay off first. If you really feel that you are in a financial hole and want out, begin paying for everything in cash while paying down your credit cards. This may be inconvenient, but it does put you in control of your finances.

Step 3: Figure out how much money, monthly or in total, you need to pursue your Future Picture. For example, if you want to go back to school, find out the monthly and total costs. Include *all* likely expenses and determine how much you need up front.

Step 4: Research your financial options. This includes grants, loans, scholarships, and work-study programs for school. Identify which options best fit your starting point.

Step 5: Create a financial plan based on all this information. If you have credit-card debt, determine how long it will take you to pay it off. If your apartment lease is up, consider moving into a smaller place or getting roommates. If you're married and have a stay-at-home spouse, find a home-based business for him or her to run.

Step 5.5: Put your financial game plan into action! If this means you need a loan, apply for a loan from *ten* different banks or other lending organizations. If this means you need investors, write a business plan and start setting up investor meetings. If this means working two jobs so you can go back to grad school, get those jobs. See your future as priceless, and you won't put too high a price tag on your success!

6. The Physical Excuse

Sean's story says it all when it comes to dealing with physical challenges. Such challenges prove that life is not fair or easy—but *you get to choose* how you deal with them.

Typical Defeatist Declaration: I'm just not attractive enough (strong enough, fit enough) to realize my dreams.

From the X-Cuse Files:

Since he was a kid, Doug, twenty-nine, always wanted to become a chef. Whenever he gets the chance he cooks for friends and family or tries out a new restaurant. He always jokes with his buddies about how great it would be to cook full-time and maybe, one day, work his way up to having his own TV cooking show. He talks about how fun it would be to constantly create new recipes and share them with the world. As much as the thought excites him, he isn't willing to enroll in his local culinary school, because he lost two fingers in a childhood accident and he fears people will stare at him. What's more he believes that no producer at a cooking show would ever be interested in a host with missing fingers. His injured hand has become the excuse he uses to not chase his dream—even though he already has proved himself to be an outstanding cook.

Moving Beyond the Physical Excuse

Step 1: Recognize that *you* choose how your physical challenge affects your life. No one can choose for you. You can turn your physical challenges into permission to hate life or a reason to love life even more. You make that choice, and then you live that choice.

Step 2: Write down three reasons why your physical challenge makes you stronger, wiser, or more resilient. Have you become a better listener? Are you more patient with others?

Do you have talents other people don't? Do you have knowledge in a niche area?

Step 3: Identify two people who you think are role models for the success and lifestyle you want. Find out what challenges they have had to overcome to get where they are. Use them as real-life examples in times when you question your own abilities.

Step 4: Join two not-for-profit organizations that can help you reach your dreams. One of these organizations should focus on assisting people with your physical challenge. Attend its meetings and take on a leadership position. The second organization should align with your Future Picture. This could be a nursing, architecture, or volunteer association. Attend their meetings and take on a leadership position. Through these two organizations, you will open incredible doors for networking, finding resources, and creating the opportunities you need to move forward.

Step 5: Design your own Reality Check Challenge. Create it in a way that forces you to confront your physical challenge head-on. Learn how to ski, complete a marathon, or earn an advanced psychology degree. Enter a public speaking competition, volunteer for a food drive, or start a business from your home. Choose to turn your physical challenge into a *natural advantage!*

7. The Time Excuse

Once I asked a room full of aspiring collegiate entrepreneurs how much more time Bill Gates had in a day than they did. Someone yelled out, "As much time as he wants. He invented the clock on my computer." While this got a laugh, it made the point that everyone has the same number of minutes in a day. It's *what you do* with your daily allotment of minutes that determines whether you run in circles or take the lead.

When you make "not having enough time" your favorite

excuse, what you're really saying is that you're not good at managing your time and priorities. This is especially true if you've made a career out of cramming, procrastinating, over-committing, and being in a hurry. If you're not careful, your crazy schedule can lead to you working hard making everyone happy—except yourself.

Typical Defeatist Declaration: I just don't have enough time to chase my dreams.

From the X-Cuse Files:

Danny is a single dad of three kids: two girls and one boy. He's talked and talked about writing a book based on his consulting expertise. He thinks being an author would allow him to help more people and enable him to spend more time with his kids. But whenever he gets close to actually writing the book, he hides behind his ready-made excuse: "I have no time." Even though his three kids are at school and other activities eight hours a day nine months a year, Danny is convinced he can't spare fifteen minutes a day to work on his book. As long as Danny claims he has no time to write his book, he forces himself to travel to make a living which, ironically, takes him away from the kids he loves so much.

Moving Beyond the Time Excuse

Step 1: Figure out where your time is going. For one week, write down what you do each day in thirty-minute increments. Then determine the average amount of time you invest in each major area of your life *each day*.

Step 2: Compare this use of your time to your Future Picture. Are you giving yourself enough time to connect with your family? Are you giving yourself enough time to be physically fit? Are you giving yourself enough time to rest and relax? If one area of your life monopolizes up all your time (such as work), then set a boundary for how much time you are willing to work each day or week. *Big hint:* There will *always* be more work to be done. However, when you make time to enjoy a gorgeous sunset with your best friend you are experiencing a truly once-in-a-lifetime event!

Step 3: When you see where your time is going, pay attention to your less-rewarding, time-consuming habits. Trade these unfulfilling habits for something more meaningful. Even setting aside thirty minutes for running on Wednesdays instead of working late or going to happy hour will make you feel more in control.

Step 4: Set aside some "me time" every day—even if it's just twenty minutes. Me time gives you the space each day to get refocused on your own well-being. Me time allows you to appreciate and build on the success you create. Me time keeps you centered on what makes your life special.

Step 5: Take a vacation *every* year. This should be the first thing you write on every calendar you buy. Having a vacation planned gives you something to look forward to during your most stressful times. It also ensures you take a much needed break from rushing around every year.

Step 6: Set aside thirty minutes, three times a week to focus on building your real-world education. Only thirty minutes, three times a week leads to seventy-five or more hours of time you have dedicated to personal growth annually. These thirty-minute blocks are perfect for exploring opportunities, reading an exciting book, or meeting with your mentor. Control your schedule, and you will succeed right on time!

BUT . . . OF COURSE

After reading this laundry list of excuses, it's obvious you can find something or someone to blame for whatever is not going right in your life. However, hiding behind excuses only makes your situation worse. Excuses give away your power to choose a wise response to your situation that ultimately moves you forward. Excuses keep you from solving your problems and growing stronger in the process. When you finally choose to let go of your excuses, you free yourself to grab on to your dreams.

Sean proves this perfectly. He could have used his osteogenesis imperfecta as an excuse to be bitter, depressed, and play it safe. Instead, he uses his physical condition to spread his powerful message, "Life is full of pain. Suffering is optional. Excuses only extend your suffering."

Life will not always be fair, but *you* control how you deal with it. Choose not to make excuses, and instead, use your power to create solutions that move you ahead!

INSTANT MESSAGE

► You can create excuses or you can create solutions, but not both at the same time.

► Several excuses that erode your potential are mental self-sabotage.

► When you let go of your excuses, they can no longer hold you back!

BOUNCED: I would like to succeed, but . . .

CASHED: I will succeed—no ifs, ands, or buts about it.

ONLINE: Watch Sean talk about dealing with excuses at **www.myrealitycheckbounced.com/book**

9

THE FEAR FACTOR

> You cannot outrun your fears.
> To demolish them you must
> run through them.

REALITY-CHECK MOMENT—
I WANT TO MAKE A BIG CHANGE,
BUT I'M SCARED OF THE CONSEQUENCES.

In Chapter 2, I talked about settling for safe. This decision to avoid big risks in the real world is a major reason many twentysomethings choose relationships, careers, lifestyles, and goals that are ultimately not that satisfying. These people are afraid of failure or afraid of rejection or afraid of the unknown, so they choose the path of least resistance and hope for the best. Unfortunately, the playing-it-safe path is often paved with boredom and tedium, and from the get-go you know in your heart it will never truly satisfy, but you do it anyway. Are you on a safe but unfulfilling path like this or are you bravely pursuing your dreams in spite of your fears?

Stephen is a prime example of someone who settled for safe. His career started off like a rocket. He graduated from a prestigious university, became a budding McKinsey consultant, then a prodigy financier, and then a dot-com millionaire and CFO at age twenty-six. That dot-com adventure was amazing while it lasted. Money fell from the sky like candy from overstuffed piñatas. The business ventures Stephen was involved in raised more than $90,000,000 of investment capital. And he lived the lavish lifestyle to prove it.

True, Stephen's start-ups never made a profit, but back then, whose did? It wasn't about profitability; it was about IPOs and LBOs and MBOs. One night, Stephen was so excited about the launch of his newest company that he dyed his jet black hair bright blue. The color matched his new company's bold strategy for reaching hip teenage girls.

In hindsight, Stephen should have seen the end coming when the blue hair arrived. He knew how to value businesses. He knew market cycles—in fact, that was his specialty. But the fast money and over-the-top lifestyle seduced his better judgment.

Reality struck when he saw once high-flying dot-com executives stop bragging about their stock options and start selling their office furniture. As CFO, Stephen knew that his current start-up's expenses were eating through cash like a tapeworm. In years past, there had always been new investors with new money to save the day. Not this time.

The bubble was bursting. Those who had gotten out at the top were fabulously rich. Those still in the dot-com business, like Stephen, were trapped with worthless stock options and the walls caving in. With growing expenses and no new investor's money to his rescue, Stephen saw the end coming. He felt as if he were trying to outrun a train while wearing sandals. Smack. It was over.

Within one year, every highly touted company that Stephen started or helped start collapsed in on itself. He took the loss of jobs, money, friendships, and perspective *personally*. He should have known better. How could he have been so naive?

He got so down on himself he was convinced even God hated him.

That's what led Stephen back home. He thought spending a little time reconnecting with his family would help him get his head on straight. It didn't. How could he relax on his parents' couch watching TV shows about the rich and famous when just a year before he had been one of them? The depth of his fall plagued him. *Every* job on his résumé in the last five years was with a now-defunct company. He had just turned thirty years old and felt as if he were starting all over.

Making it worse, his previous business heroes were being paraded in handcuffs on the evening news or were themselves looking for jobs. He didn't want to be one of them. He never again wanted to feel the pain and humiliation of failure. This fear gradually ate at Stephen's independence and courage until he succumbed and accepted a safe eight to five j-o-b.

FROM DOT-COM MILLIONAIRE TO DILBERT

His new job was purchasing small companies and combining them together to be sold as one larger company. His position was highly paid, and he had a big title. He should have been thrilled, but he wasn't. Every time he paid an entrepreneur wearing worn-out blue jeans eight figures to buy her business his inner entrepreneur burned. He wanted to be his own boss and once again control his destiny, but his fear of failure was just too great.

After six months as a well-paid but uninspired employee, Stephen began feeling extremely restless at work. This time, though, the stress was not from his fear of failure. The stress was coming from something much deeper: his identity.

Stephen was starting to see that his current job was in conflict with everything he believed in and stood for. Sure, his job was high paying, but it was forcing him to turn his back on what, deep down, he knew to be true about himself. *Stephen was born to be an entrepreneur*. It wasn't about money or status—it was about being your own boss and creating something from the ground up. Pursuing anything else, even a high-paying job, was a compromise inherently destined to be unsatisfying.

It didn't matter to Stephen if he owned a company with a thousand employees or just him. It didn't matter if his face was on the cover of *Forbes* or simply in a picture frame hanging in his mom's living room. All that mattered to him was to be his own boss again. He needed to start another business.

This left Stephen with *no choice* but to face his now deeply rooted fear of failure. This was more frightening than any business problem he had ever encountered because this challenge was *inside him*. His fear could not be outsourced or overcome with better financing. To overcome his fear of failure, Stephen had to face it head-on.

ESCAPE FROM RAT-RACE HELL

Stephen forced himself to step back from his situation and see the bigger picture. In doing this he made a stunning and unexpected observation: Maybe facing failure was an integral part of being an entrepreneur?

He realized for the first time that he had failed before—many times, in fact—and he was still alive. Failure was never fun or comfortable, but it also wasn't *that* bad. He could survive it again. If anything, his previous business failures taught him *what not to do* next time.

Stephen took his first step in this new direction by calling Brian, an old college friend. He told Brian that he had decided it was time to stand up for his dreams and *never* again settle for less. The more Stephen talked about daring to be great, the more Brian laughed over the phone. Brian thought, "Who was Stephen to talk about pursuing greatness? He was a repeat repeat repeat repeat repeat failure!"

Two months later, Stephen and Brian had both quit their high-paying jobs to become business partners. They launched their new decidedly low-tech business from a shared desk and phone line in the extra bedroom of Stephen's house.

I met with Stephen shortly after he had shared his story of repeat business failures with a classroom of college business students. He joked that the more details he shared, the fewer notes the students took. Apparently, they couldn't believe someone could have over $90,000,000 in losses on his résumé *before turning thirty*. What most shocked the students was learning Stephen had the audacity to launch another business.

One student finally asked Stephen the question on everyone's mind, "Aren't you scared to start another business? I mean, every business you've ever started in your entire life has failed. What if you fail again?" Stephen shrugged, "If I fail again, I'll just have to start another business. It's part of what makes having a dream so great. If you fail, you get back up and you keep trying. There is no why or how. You simply get back up and try again until you make it happen."

Stephen's answer was right on. So was his decision to face his fears by starting another business. At press time, his low-tech rental business was on track to make *Inc. Magazine*'s list of the fastest-growing privately held companies in America.

FEARS ARE HUMAN

Like Stephen, you have fears. *Everyone* has fears. Fears are natural. Fears are human. You may even share some common twentysomething fears such as these:
- Never being able to pay off your credit-card or college debt
- Marrying the wrong person
- Living on your own

- Losing your job
- Not finding your bigger purpose

But fear is not necessarily *always* a bad thing. Since the beginning of humankind, fear has played an important role in alerting people to avoid potential danger. Thank goodness our ancient ancestors were prewired with fear. This acted like a physical alarm, helping them evade danger so they could live longer and make more babies. This internal alarm was essential to staying alive in a world full of never-before-seen creatures and experiences.

Back then there was no Internet to find out if a certain snakebite was deadly. There was no 911 to call if you were being followed by a stranger. There definitely were no laser-guided weapons for a preemptive strike. When our ancestors unexpectedly came across a grizzly bear, fear would tell them, "Warning! Warning! Warning! Fight or run! Fight or run!" Then our ancestors would flee, fight, or fake death.

In the modern world, you probably won't confront a grizzly bear on your morning commute—although a sixteen-year-old driving an SUV might be just as dangerous! But you still have the same fear-based alarm pulsing through your body to help you avoid potential harm. You feel this alarm go off when you're surprised from behind, when you instinctively jump out of the path of an oncoming car, and when you try your best to protect those you love.

BEWARE FANTASY FEARS

Your internal alarm system was designed to keep you safe in a world filled with potential dangers. However, if you allow your fears to run wild in your imagination they can end up actually *keeping you from your most important, meaningful dreams.*

How so? When your fears become so strong that they steal your courage, creativity, and resilience they have become *fantasy fears*. These irrational, overgrown fears keep you from taking the calculated steps and corresponding risks necessary to get where you want to go. In extreme cases, your fantasy fears can grow into phobias that can imprison you in your own mind.

People suffering from phobias can become so terrified that they can't sleep, go outside, or throw away their trash. I knew one person who was so scared of leaving her house that she never went outside for ten years! When her family finally convinced her to leave they were shocked to find that she had saved every newspaper and piece of mail she received during her self-imposed confinement. If you or someone you know might have a phobia, get professional help. That mental maze is not a challenge you want to face alone.

For most of you, though, you don't have anything close to a phobia. Your fears are much more in line with Stephen's. His fear of failure started small and grew as his business failures did. He then hid from this fear of failure by taking a safe job. Settling for this safe path only gave his fear more room and time to grow. He finally reached a breaking point. He could continue following his fear toward safety and dissatisfaction or he could choose to stand up once again for his dreams. At that life-defining moment, he chose his dream of being an entrepreneur over his fear of failure. This put him back on a riskier, less predictable path, but it was the most direct route to his feeling alive with purpose.

How did Stephen find the courage to roll up his sleeves and face his fear? The same way you can. He acknowledged his fear, and *he took action in spite of it!* This gave his passion for being an entrepreneur the chance to overtake his insecurities, which came from his previous failures. In little time he was back in control of his confidence, direction, and future.

For many of you, your fears are *just strong enough* that they keep you from chasing your bigger, more meaningful dreams. Each day you choose not to confront these fears is one more day you add to their strength. Why? By not confronting your fears you silently show that *on some level* you believe they are accurate. This gives your fears the room to grow stronger and become more difficult to break.

HEAD GAMES

You've seen what your imagination can do *for* you. Here are three examples of what it can do *to* you:

1. During high school you ask your teacher a question during class. The other students think it's dumb and laugh at you. Your imagination could turn that experience into a fantasy *fear based on rejection* that keeps you from asking questions when you need help. Not asking questions could lead to you not asking for help at your job, which causes you to make a big mistake and ultimately get fired. This mistake would have been easy to avoid if only you weren't irrationally afraid to ask for help.
2. Your dad gets laid off from his job when you were a kid, so the bank forecloses on your house. Your imagination could turn that bad experience into a fantasy *fear based on failure* that keeps you from ever buying your own house. Not buying your own house could keep you from one of the best financial investments you can make. You end up staying a renter for life when the entire time you could have been a home owner!
3. You are crushed when something unexpectedly bad happens

to your first love. Your imagination could turn that experience into a fantasy *fear based on the unknown* that keeps you emotionally distant from those you most care about. This could lead you to never opening up to another person, so you miss out on experiencing true love.

You know your fears are overdeveloped and limiting your progress when they keep you from meeting new people, taking on challenges, and pursuing your true identity. If your fears remain unchallenged, you can find yourself stuck on an unsatisfying path because it's the only one that seems safe. You eventually start using every excuse in the book (see Chapter 8) to mask your deeper fear.

BOUNCED: My fears keep me on a path that is not completely satisfying.

CASHED: I *feel* the fear, but do it anyway.

CHALLENGE FEAR WITH REALITY

To push beyond the grip of your deepest fears, you must challenge them with a heavy dose of reality. Nothing deflates overgrown fears as fast as contrary real-life experience. This type of experience forces your mind to see that your irrational, limiting fears are only a figment of your imagination.

With each fear you put in check by challenging it with reality, you take its power. You'll soon feel a new sense of freedom, resilience, and confidence. When you conquer your deepest fears, you prove to yourself that your mind is on your side.

Go ahead and start putting your fears in check *now*. List

the three fears you believe most keep you from your Future Picture:

- **Fear 1:** _____
- **Fear 2:** _____
- **Fear 3:** _____

A few real-life twentysomething examples of fear:
- I'm afraid to ask the women I like to go on a date.
- I'm afraid to ask my boss for a promotion.
- I'm afraid to move to a new town.
- I'm afraid to start my own business.
- I'm afraid to trust people.
- I'm afraid to show my body at the gym.
- I'm afraid of making a big mistake.
- I'm afraid of going to graduate school.

You may not want to put your fears in writing, so I'll share mine to show you that you're not alone. Here are the three fears that first came to my mind when I went through this process:

Fear 1: Missing out on once-in-a-lifetime events with family and friends.

Fear 2: Dying before I enjoy the Future Picture I've worked hard to create.

Fear 3: Being unable to physically or mentally take care of myself.

Looking over the three biggest fears you listed (or that came to your mind) do you think they stem from a specific event or experience in your past? Is one of your fears related to a rough time in your childhood? Is one of your fears from hanging out with too many overachievers? Or are your fears more a result of watching too much reality TV?

Whatever your fears' origin, they grew stronger as you left them unchallenged to run wild in your imagination. Now these fears affect how you see yourself, the world, and the risks you're willing to take to live your all-important Future Picture. You must move beyond your fears, *and the artificial boundaries they create*, so you have space to go after what you most want.

FACING YOUR FEARS

Just as I identified the seven excuses that erode potential, I put together a list of the most common twentysomething fears. I call these the *Three Faces of Fear*. Conquer these three fears and you free yourself to choose whatever path most brings meaning and excitement to your life.

FACE OF FEAR 1: FEAR OF FAILURE

Fear of failure is the number one fear keeping twentysomethings from living with more meaning, passion, and purpose. Fear of failure is toxic to your courage because it keeps you from taking the risks necessary to get ahead. The earlier this fear takes root, the more damage it inflicts through lost time and opportunity. If your fear of failure remains unchallenged, your imagination can become your own worst enemy. You can end up going through life doing everything possible to play it safe rather than doing everything possible to live your most meaningful dreams.

Typical fear of failure Statement: I can't do that; I might lose.

How does your mind make the risk of failure so terrifying that you will give up pursuing your most inspiring dreams? You make failure *personal*.

Fear in Action

Maurine knows how scary it feels to make failure personal. In her second semester at nursing school, she got behind and wasn't able to catch up. She failed one class and was so afraid she might not have what it takes to be a nurse, that she took off the next semester and seriously considered not going back. A friend finally convinced her that all she needed to succeed was to take fewer classes each semester, which is what she eventually did. Now she's a nurse and she loves it. However, if Maurine's friend had not helped her face her fear of failure, she might have given up her lifelong dream—all because she failed one class!

Maurine's mistake was that she made her failure personal. She let one failed class mean that she wasn't cut out for her dream. Making failure personal adds emotion to your setbacks, which crushes your confidence, creativity, and self-esteem. One-time setbacks can grow into lifelong stumbling blocks. Short-term missteps become unrecoverable mistakes. When you make failure personal you take the wind out of your sails and can become so paralyzed with fear that you can't chart a new course.

To keep from making failure personal, you have to separate *who you are* from *what you do*. When you separate who you are from what you do, you create room to see all your failures—and you are likely to have many—as temporary. This approach helps you learn from them and move on, even if you have to stop and regroup. By separating who you are from what you do, you can persist through the most trying failure because you see failure for what it is: a test of your commitment to living your Future Picture.

Here are some examples of how you can separate yourself from failure:

- If you flunk out of college, you're not a failure, *your approach to college was*. Figure out what you can do differently next time and reenroll.
- If you start a business and it goes bankrupt, you're not a failure, *your business model was*. Research how to improve your business model so your next venture is a home run.
- If you have a relationship and it falls apart, you're not a failure, *the relationship was*. Identify what went wrong and work on it so during your next go-round you both get what you want.

As frustrating as failure can feel, it doesn't signify that you're worthless, a bad person, or that your ideas are without merit. Failure is simply a by-product of progress. At worst, failure is an intensely educational experience that teaches you a valuable lesson. At best, failure is the perfect setup for finding new solutions to old problems so you get what you want quicker.

In fact, many of the greatest inventions, social advancements, and civil rights, came from people who failed repeatedly—and often in public! They didn't give up and neither should you.

Let me say it this way: if you're not failing, *you're not pushing yourself to your limit*. You have further to go to find out what you are truly made of and prove to yourself what you are capable of achieving.

TO CONQUER FEAR OF FAILURE

1. **See yourself as an underdog.** Underdogs never quit, no matter how intense the peer pressure, physical obstacle, or emotional stress. Think of the 2004 Red Sox. If they had

quit when it looked hopeless, Boston might have had to wait another eighty-six years for a World Series victory.

2. **Don't hide from who you are.** Write down every reason you can think of that proves why you can, should, and will succeed. Ask friends and family for their thoughts, too. Just as Stephen did, get clear that success is who you are!

3. **Know that baby steps will eventually complete a marathon.** Each day, take one step forward that contradicts your fear of failure. For example, if you fear meeting new people, make it a point to introduce yourself to one stranger every day. Keep track of your baby steps toward freedom so you see you're moving forward.

4. **When the wind gets knocked out of you, let it go!** The fear of failure keeps you from learning by making your self-worth hostage to previous failures. Choose not to make your setbacks personal, and this can't happen. When you see failure as temporary, you create room to get up and get going.

5. **Keep the faith.** Doubt empowers fear, faith destroys doubt. Believe in your dreams with all your heart and you can walk through your scariest fear.

FACE OF FEAR 2: FEAR OF REJECTION

Fear of rejection can do even more damage to your spirit than fear of failure because when you fear rejection you can't ask for help! Until you confront the fear of rejection, you risk rejecting your dreams in an effort *to avoid rejection*. You must conquer this fear before your fantasy of feeling alone becomes your reality. The world has plenty of loving, accepting, kind people who are ready and willing to help you if you will only ask.

Typical Fear of Rejection Statement: I'm too scared to speak in front of a group.

Fear In Action:

Juanita always wanted to be a youth minister. The problem is she was terrified of public speaking. She was afraid the audience might not understand her accent (she was born in Mexico) or that they would question her knowledge. Because of these fears she would never volunteer to lead the youth worship at her church. One Sunday, the regular youth minister got sick at the last minute and asked her to step in and lead the service. It went so well that one week later she was named assistant youth minister!

To get past fear of rejection, you must see that *rejection is not about you*. This may sound corny, but it's true. Rejection never comes from you—*it always comes from someone else*. Rejection is always about the *other* person or organization deciding you're not the right fit for him, his needs, or his objectives.

People or groups that reject you do so based on *their* past experiences and current biases. This has nothing to do with who you are or what makes you special. This has everything to do with what *has* and *has not* worked for them. You simply don't fit into *someone else's* beliefs of what works for him.

When someone rejects you, for whatever reason, you have a choice. You can either change yourself to fit his criteria, or you can continue being who you are.

If you do change to fit someone else's desires, be sure the change doesn't betray your core identity. If it does, at some point, your true self will break through your charade. If you're not willing to change to fit other people's wishes, then you're destined to face even more rejection. Why? Because when you live for what makes you feel most alive and happy, you're bound to make people with a different view feel uncomfortable! Your attitude and ideas will make them feel nervous, threatened, jealous, or insecure.

When these people reject you, remember: Not everyone

will like you the way you are, but for these people it's *their* loss. As long as you stay true to who you are and what makes you happy, you have the most important acceptance of all.

When you're ready to face your fear of rejection, your approach should be similar to that of your fear of failure. Choose to separate *who you are* from *those who rejected you*. This allows you to stay true to who you are and live for what most brings meaning to your life.

Here are some examples of how to separate yourself from rejection:

- If you apply for admission to an exclusive graduate program and are denied, you were not a failure; *your application was*. Find a program that wants you the way you are or learn from the experience and apply again.

- If you ask someone to go on a date and you get turned down, you were not a failure; *your technique was*. Decide whether you really want to go out with that person. If you do, try a different technique to get a different result.

- If you apply for a business loan from your bank and are rejected, you were not a failure; *your business plan was*. Determine if you actually need the loan; if so, improve your business plan and apply for the loan at three other banks.

Distancing *who you are* from *those who reject you* creates the space you need to respond *in your own best interests*. You can choose to try a new approach and create a new result. Or you can choose to continue doing what you've been doing and persist until you get what you want.

The key is that rejection will not permanently halt your progress as long as you stay true to your path. You may have to face one hundred nos to get the yes you've been working hard for, but *you will* get it when you are passionate about where you are going.

TO CONQUER FEAR OF REJECTION

1. **Recognize rejection is part of progress.** *Everyone* gets rejected; some just hide it better. See all rejection as one step closer to your goal. As long as you don't throw in the towel, all rejections are temporary.

2. **Put the odds in your favor.** Track how many nos it takes for you to get a yes. As you build your skills, you will see fewer nos between each yes!

3. **Become a rejection detector.** When rejected, ask *why*. People and organizations reject for *their* reasons. Sometimes these are valid and sometimes these are fluff. Pay attention to the valid reasons and ignore the fluff.

4. **Get a clue.** The valid reasons why you get rejected provide clues for what to do differently to get a different result. If you want this different result, incorporate these clues into your next attempt.

5. **Call the help desk.** Identify two or three friends who have proved their ability to overcome rejection. If you get rejected and start getting down on yourself, call them for inspiration. Nothing soothes rejection like unconditional acceptance.

FACE OF FEAR 3: FEAR OF THE UNKNOWN

Events, situations, and other stuff you never plan for, want, or expect *will happen*. It's not *if*, but *when*. To deal with this, you need to be prepared but not paranoid. Fear of the unknown pushes you toward paranoia and playing it safe rather than being prepared, confident, and persistent. If this fear grows unchallenged, you can become so concerned about "what might happen" that you make *nothing* happen.

Typical Fear of the Unknown Statement: I would never take that risk. Who knows what could happen?!

Fear In Action

Luis is a loud, charismatic twenty-one-year-old. Several of his old high school buddies wanted him to go to Europe for a week, and he flat out refused to go. He said anyone foolish enough to travel overseas is going to get abducted by terrorists no matter where they went. His friends kept teasing him about his fear until he finally gave in and bought his ticket to Europe. After his first full day in London—jet lag and all—he laughed about how he actually felt safer in London than where he grew up!

Fear of the unknown is powerful because it is tied to your biological aversion to pain and loss. When you have an over-size fear of the unknown your imagination highlights all the horrible things that *might* happen if you take a certain path. It's as if a scary movie were playing in your head over and over telling you not to make certain choices necessary to reaching your Future Picture because you could end up as the lead story on the six o'clock news. The stronger this fear grows, the more it disconnects you from reality.

When all your options appear unacceptably risky, fear of the unknown has scared you into living defensively—the exact opposite of what you need to have the courage to reach for your Future Picture. The earlier fear of the unknown grips your imagination, the earlier in life you will be forced to settle for playing it safe and remaining unfulfilled.

To overcome fear of the unknown, you must confront your out-of-control bad dreams with the most powerful tool available for calming overactive imaginations: reality. Countering your imaginary worst-case scenarios with realistic choices that create tangible outcomes retrains your mind to see that your future *is not predetermined* to be bad or painful. You begin to see that your future is shaped by your actions today—which *you* control—so you, *not your overactive imagination*, determine you future.

By consistently adding a healthy dose of reality to your scary daydreams about what could happen in the future, you force your mind to see all the potential good stuff that lies ahead. Over time, this will make your future look and feel brighter. You'll become more calm, confident, and levelheaded about the path you have chosen.

Many twentysomethings I interviewed struggled with fear of the unknown in some way, but they usually expressed it as, "Sure I would like to do ____, but what if ____ happens?" Here's how to get a more positive grip on reality:

1. **Research and talk to people in the know.** Why do you think fortune-tellers ask for payment in advance? Because they can't predict the future! Neither can you. But you can do research to see what's going on in the world and talk to other people who have had the experiences you seek.

2. **Get real.** Choose a path that creates outcomes you can touch, taste, smell, hear, and see. When caught in a bind use your senses to test potential outcomes to see which are real and which are only in your imagination. I knew one person who was convinced she would get robbed if she ever went downtown. Her friends finally persuaded her to go downtown with them for dinner. Afterward they walked around looking in shop windows and talking to people. Now that she has experienced what was once unknown, she thinks it was silly that she was ever afraid to go downtown!

3. **Limit your unknowns.** Choose a path with fewer unknowns until you build the confidence to take a riskier path.

4. **Imagine a positive future.** You control your imagination. Challenge negative "What if . . . ?" scenarios with positive "What if . . . ?" dreams. The more positive the future you imagine, the more positive you'll feel about your future.

5. **Create or find your safe place.** If you take a risk and experience too

much pain, retreat to your safe place and regroup. Once you feel okay again, identify what you can do differently next time and start in that direction with baby steps.

CHOOSE YOUR FUTURE PICTURE OVER YOUR FEARS

Fear may be a natural part of life, but it shouldn't keep you from living. Get real about the fears that hold you back. Choose to face them head-on. Challenge them until *they* are afraid of *you*!

INSTANT MESSAGE

► Everyone has fears; they're a biological alarm for keeping you safe.
► If your fears grow unchallenged, they will eventually steal your confidence.
► Overcome your fears, and you turn that emotion into your power!

BOUNCED: My fears keep me on a path that is not completely satisfying.

CASHED: I *feel* the fear, but do it anyway.

ONLINE: Read more about Stephen's new business at **www.myrealitycheckbounced.com/book**

10

LIFE IN THE BALANCE

> What you do with your time shows
> what you most prize.

REALITY-CHECK MOMENT:
SURE, I'M SUCCESSFUL, BUT I HAVE NO LIFE!

Are you always in a rush, running from home to work to play to work to food to work to friends to work to bed and then to repeat the cycle? Maybe you seek extra projects to take on during weekends and never get off your cell phone, Blackberry, or laptop. You find comfort juggling more then what you could ever possibly accomplish. You rush and rush *but never seem to catch* whatever it is you're chasing. And when you actually take a few rare free seconds to stop and take inventory of your life, you realize that you're completely off balance. You've been eating the same greasy take-out food for weeks; you haven't called your mom or your friends for months; you work so many hours that people think you actually live in your office. In short, you're busy but miserable.

For Sara, twenty-seven, entry into the real world was one most young professionals only dream about. It started when she landed the prized sales position every marketing graduate at her top-tier business school wanted. Her new multibillion-dollar employers were well known, well established, and well respected. Getting hired by them was a huge vote of confidence.

Their famed training program paired Sara with the best and the brightest from premier universities across the globe. As one elite group, these new hires were trained by current executives to become future executives.

After completing training, Sara's first assignment was as a field marketing representative. She received a company car, expense account, and great salary with *lots* of benefits. In exchange for all this, her boss expected only one thing—her complete dedication to making their company's products fly off the shelves of retailers in her territory.

Sara loves a challenge. She accepted this first real-world assignment with pride and enthusiasm. Her zest for work and life quickly spread to the stores in her territory. The store managers in fact looked forward to seeing her, and she loved helping them sell more of her company's stuff.

Sales in her territory began rising in the second quarter after she took over. This was proof of her success learning the market, building key relationships, and working those relationships from sunrise to sunset. Sara didn't mind. It was her job. She was on a path straight to the executive level, possibly before age thirty.

After six months working in the field, Sara's boss was so impressed he asked her to transfer to their company's national headquarters in a different state. There she would work side by side with division executives. She would learn how to create the products she so effectively marketed. Along with a hefty increase in salary, she would get to travel overseas—a big bonus for someone who had not traveled much. The opportunity was so good she didn't hesitate to say yes!

The promotion turned out better than Sara imagined. She

was whisked from Asia to Arizona for business trips. She stayed at beautiful resorts. She worked with smart people solving complex problems. One night she even sat next to the company CEO during dinner. He wanted *her opinion* on what the company could do to be more successful!

Her most exciting responsibility was being put in charge of taking a new product from concept to completion. This responsibility included everything from visiting the factory in China where the product would be produced to creating the marketing campaign for releasing the product. It was amazing. Sara was only twenty-three years old and launching her own product that her mom could buy at the grocery store!

PERSONAL LIFE—R.I.P.

In all the excitement, Sara became skilled at working ridiculously long hours. Friends called less and less because they knew she would be too busy to return their calls. Boyfriends became a thing of the past as her work ran later into the evenings. But she didn't mind staring at her laptop into the wee hours; she had so much to do *she didn't have time to care*.

After a year working at her company's national headquarters, Sara was transferred to Chicago. This would be the third state in which she had lived in a year and a half, but again she didn't mind. She was on the fast track to corporate stardom. And Chicago sounded fun.

Sara got a corporate apartment a few blocks from Michigan Avenue. She figured the location would motivate her to get out of the office and build a social life. She was wrong. Her new job brought more responsibilities and even longer work hours. In her mind, it was still worth it. She was just paying her dues like her boss had done before her and his boss had done before him.

Sara began to practically live at her office. She quit exercising, her one daily escape—because who had time for exercise when she hadn't even unpacked her moving boxes? As long as Sara stayed in a hurry, she felt as if she were on top of the world or fast approaching it.

Who could blame her? She was making great money, working for a big-name company, and earning prestigious assignments. She was in the eye of an adrenaline tornado. As long as she had more to do than she could possibly accomplish, life was grand. It was only in the rare moments when she stopped sprinting that her spirit dropped. Her boss helped her avoid this by assigning additional responsibilities whenever Sara got close to catching up.

A WAKE-UP CALL

At 8:30 P.M. on a frigid Friday in February, Sara's tornado spun apart. She was at her office, as usual, working on a report that had to be completed by midnight. Her cell phone rang. She grabbed it from her jacket pocket and checked the caller ID. It was her mom, so she answered. The voice on the line was definitely her mom's, but it was hard to hear because of the loud music in the background.

Concentrating, Sara finally understood what her mom was saying. She was at a restaurant in Florida and Alan Jackson, Sara's favorite singer, was eating dinner there. To everyone's surprise, he spontaneously decided to put on a show. Sara's mom held the phone in the air so Sara could hear Alan Jackson singing "It's Five O'Clock Somewhere."

Sara smiled, momentarily lost in the music. Then her mom told her she had to go because she was about to dance! Sara said good-bye and looked out her large office window at the twinkling lights of Chicago. She could see cars streaming along the highway. She imagined the people in those cars heading to dinner with friends, a ballgame with family, or a movie with a date. She was alone looking at spreadsheets at 8:30 on a Friday night.

That was the moment. Sara saved her work and turned off her computer. One by one she picked up the pictures on her desk and looked at the memories. She would come back for the pictures later. Tonight she was going home for a long over-due night with her friends.

For the first time since landing her prestigious job, Sara turned off the lights in her office without feeling guilty about having more work to do. She was starting to see that being in a hurry wasn't necessarily success, but being happy with your life was. It was finally five o'clock for Sara.

A month later, Sara, the previously nonstop high-flying star-to-be, was on a lazy beach in south Florida. I know be-cause she called me. She and her mom were working on their suntans. A few job offers were trickling in, but she wasn't rushing into anything. She needed to reconnect with herself first, so she could find out what to do with her life *next*.

Note: At the time of this writing, Sara has been out of the corporate sprint for one year. She tried a few jobs and then settled into one that she absolutely loves: high school science teacher. It was a big cut in pay but a huge raise in fulfillment.

BEWARE THE BUSY BINGERS

For many twentysomethings like Sara, being busy is their drug. Being busy makes them feel good on the outside because it keeps them from looking inside. The busier they are, the more important, valued, and successful they feel. As over-whelming as their life can appear to an outsider, they refuse vacations because they can't stand the thought of just hanging out doing nothing on a beach for a week.

These overworked twentysomethings care more about staying busy than being fulfilled because, the truth is, fulfillment comes from *having a life* not from a twenty-four-hour job.

I'm embarrassed to admit it, but I know this because two years ago I was living in a hurry. I was twenty-five years old and wrapped up in my career and the image of success that I thought being busy projected. I felt I had to prove what I could achieve. I'd even pull all-nighters to make sure important projects were done *my way*.

I lived for my job 24/7, 365. This was fine until I started getting sick. It got to the point that I was getting sick about once a month. It was never some horrible sickness, but I would catch a cold and feel run down for a week. No matter how much I slept on airplanes or gobbled vitamin C, I never felt totally healthy.

I don't know if I was getting sick because I was shaking so many people's hands after seminars; if I was simply getting older, and my body couldn't hold up like it once did; if I was eating too much prepackaged airport food; or if I just needed more time in my own bed. But I could not deny I was feeling off my game and it was only getting worse.

When the circles under my eyes got so dark that strangers asked if I was feeling okay, I swallowed my youthful pride and went to my doctor. I didn't like what he said so I went to a different doctor. When he said the same thing I quit being stubborn and listened.

The doctors said I was getting sick and *staying sick* because I was pushing myself so hard. I was not giving my body time to recover. My stressed-out lifestyle was making my body weaker and weaker. The result would be my eventual burnout or physical collapse. They said I was a poster child for the overworked young professional who stresses themselves straight into a heart attack before turning forty.

I was hoping they would tell me I could heal myself by eating more spinach or switching multivitamins, but they said a temporary remedy wouldn't work. They said I needed to cancel all my appointments and sit on my butt for two weeks. They said that a two week stay-at-home vacation would help me see how to reprioritize my life.

SANITY TO THE RESCUE

Being told to stay home for two weeks didn't sound like vacation to me. In fact, it sounded like house arrest. But when my mom found out what the doctors said, I had no choice.

After running full speed for so long, I didn't know how to slow down and get my life in order. So I went to my mentors for advice. At the time, I had four mentors (whom I found through the steps outlined in Chapter 6). These mentors had already achieved incredible success in different areas of their life and were helping me do the same. I figured they would have something profound to tell me. Instead, *they laughed*.

Not like someone laughing at you, but like someone laughing with you because you both tripped on the same step when no one was looking. I soon learned that every one of my well-respected mentors was a recovering workaholic or lifeaholic (people who work hard *and* play hard). One of my mentors did not alter his crazy work schedule until his second heart attack. Another waited until his third divorce, and another postponed a more peaceful life until he unexpectedly received full custody of his two elementary-age kids.

I was surprised to learn that my mentors had gone through the same physical and mental exhaustion I was experiencing. Some bottomed out in their late twenties, but most were in their mid-thirties when they really hit the wall. They shared how this physical and emotional defeat pushed them to get serious about how they lived the *one* life they had. All my mentors emerged stronger from their close calls with burnout, and they told me that I could, too—if I started paying attention to where I was in such a hurry to go.

My oldest mentor—he's now seventy-two years old—explained that it wasn't how many hours I worked in a day or a week. What mattered was how much time I consistently invested toward building a *life*—not just building my wallet or achievements. (This mentor still jogs every day with his wife of forty plus years!)

He explained that there was no magic formula for finding life balance. But the further out of balance I became, the shakier my health, happiness, relationships, and future would become. He said that I should listen to my doctors' warnings *now*, so I wouldn't make myself sick running past once-in-a-lifetime memories.

That's not what I wanted to hear at age twenty-five.

BOUNCED: Being extremely busy means I'm a success.

CASHED: Success is having the time to do what makes me feel most alive.

FOUR WAYS TO GET YOUR BALANCE BACK

When my mentor approached his own burnout point in his mid-thirties, he survived by changing his entire routine. He realized that to live the life he wanted his routine had to reflect his *life* priorities—not just his career priorities. He put each of his life priorities in order and then set aside time each day to be true to them. This strategy made his schedule less hectic while bringing him closer to new, important priorities: family, spirituality, and health.

Action 1. Find Your Focus

From my mentor's experience, the secret to success was to do what you must first, so you have time the rest of the day to do what you want. This was my first lesson in the power of *focus*. When you learn to focus your time and energy, you can go from hopping hurriedly in a thousand different directions to moving a thousand feet forward in one rewarding direction.

At my most burned out point, I was overwhelming myself by constantly taking on new challenges and responsibilities. I was getting distracted by unexpected phone calls, junk e-mails, and unnecessary meetings—effectively, I was hopping in too many directions. My lack of focus made it frighteningly easy for me to lose myself in a busy schedule that tore me down rather than built me up.

Once my oldest mentor helped me see that being busy rarely equals success. It was time for me to rearrange my schedule. I had to make my *quality of life* my top priority. To do this, I changed my schedule to include my Future Picture noncareer priorities such as relationships, spirituality, family, and health.

Action 2: Try the Thirty-Minute Solution

My oldest mentor then told me that a big secret toward creating the quality of life I desired was to pursue my life priorities in daily thirty-minute blocks.

Setting aside thirty minutes each day to achieve my life priorities didn't sound complicated, until I checked my calendar. I had already committed to so many meetings, events, and deadlines that thirty minutes of uninterrupted time was impossible to find! I shared this with my oldest mentor. I told him that I just didn't have the spare time to act on his time management advice. That didn't fly too well.

He said that if leaders from the president to the pope could set aside time each day for learning and peace of mind, I could, too. He also said that if my picture of the future was as important as I claimed, then I would find a way to make it happen.

Then he asked me to describe my Future Picture in detail. As I shared it with him, it became obvious to me that being crazy-busy was not part of that picture. For some reason this had never occurred to me. I was embarrassed to see that I had been running so fast I didn't notice I was running on a treadmill.

The more I thought about my situation, the more I realized I didn't want to spend the next forty years working so hard. I was already worn out and I was only twenty-five. My focus shifted from being constantly in motion to being effective with the least motion possible.

Once I took control of my schedule, I was able to create daily blocks of uninterrupted me time that aligned with my priorities. To make this precious time as beneficial as possible, I went back to my oldest mentor for advice. He told me to use the first thirty minutes as an independent study on improving myself. He said by regularly focusing on developing my attitude and skills I'd be positioned to make the most of my life. I called this first thirty minute block of me time my *Half Hour to Full Power*.

HALF-HOUR TO FULL POWER

In this Half Hour to Full Power my goal was to build my knowledge while making consistent progress in my four priority life areas: relationships, spirituality, health, and work. One habit I got into was calling a different family member each day. I had no idea how much closer this would bring me to my family. At first, it was hard to turn off my work phone for thirty minutes and focus solely on bettering myself. However, I came to cherish this thirty-minute block of me time as one of the pillars to my sanity and creativity.

The next block of thirty minutes that I could set aside was for evaluating opportunity. Once I learned how to see the world as overflowing with opportunity, I had to figure out which ones to pursue. For this I used the Six Questions for Opportunity from pages 68–70 to help me distinguish the gems from the junk.

Any extra time that I was able to set aside during the day went to other endeavors that aligned with my Future Picture: exercising, calling old friends, and reading a good book. I know from where you're sitting it may seem like devoting thirty minutes a day toward living with more balance may seem like adding unnecessary work, *but it's only thirty minutes.* That's less time per day than some of you spend deciding what to eat for dinner. And change requires effort. If thirty minutes a day for yourself is more than you're willing to commit, try setting aside thirty minutes every weekend. Once you try it, you'll adopt your own Half Hour to Full Power. I guarantee it.

Action 3: No'ing is Half the Battle

I came to terms with the fact that I was not going to simply *find* thirty minutes of free time throughout my day. I had become too much of an expert at staying busy. This block of time would be found only if I *created* it. Then I learned the most powerful word in any language for refocusing your schedule to match your life priorities: no.

This one little word gives you mastery of your schedule and allows you to reduce the stress that goes with being overcommitted. *No* also happened to be the word I least liked saying. I always felt bad turning people down when they wanted help or to just hang out. But I had to learn how to say no and stick to it. This one word was the best tool I had to regain control of my schedule and refocus it on a more meaningful lifestyle.

The first victims of my new determination to live a more balanced life were my weekly business meetings. In truth, these weren't business meetings. They were a chance to chat with a friend or adviser about what was going on in the world. We would kick around ideas, share a cup of coffee and catch up. I now understand that these business meetings were unnecessary diversions that kept me from pursuing more meaningful life priorities.

I also adopted a new philosophy about meetings that dramatically reduced my stress: If the meeting doesn't have the potential to move me closer to my Future Picture, *I don't go*. I know that sounds harsh, but so does the thought of missing the chance to sit outside on a gorgeous afternoon because I'm in a stale office talking with someone about something neither of us really cares about.

Action 4: Cut Down on Time Wasters

Next to go in my overbooked schedule was couch time. No, I'm not talking about me snuggling on the sofa with my girlfriend while watching *Oprah* (We still do that!). This was the *two hours* I was spending each day watching the news—after I'd already read about it on the Internet. I cut my news junkie habit down to thirty minutes a day.

My other big daily time waster was errands. It's amazing how much time you can waste going to the bank, grocery store, and post office, especially if you do each separately. Combining those errands into one weekly trip freed up forty-five minutes a day!

Saying no to unnecessary meetings, cutting back on the time-consuming activities that were out of line with my life priorities, and consolidating errands freed up between one and two hours in my schedule *each day*. My mentor said this would happen, and now I believe him. Spare time is never *found*, but you can *create* it!

To find what you've been in such a rush to uncover, put this Reality Check Challenge on your schedule:

REALITY CHECK CHALLENGE

GOAL: Create your own Half Hour to Full Power.
TASK: I challenge you to set aside, carve out, say no, or otherwise create thirty minutes sometime next week for you to solely focus on yourself. This block of time can replace a social event that doesn't move you closer to your purpose, a TV show you watch but don't really care about, or some other activity that is only a distraction. When you create this me time, focus on one of the ten areas outlined later in this chapter.

If you're so committed to living your Future Picture that you take the Reality Check Challenge, you'll find yourself with half an hour set aside for you next week. This blank space on your calendar is for your independent study on creating more meaning and fulfillment in your life.

You may be wondering how much value you can truly gain from a thirty-minute block of me time.

Good question. Think about it this way: devoting only thirty minutes per day toward your life priorities four times a week equals *over a hundred hours* you're investing annually toward your Future Picture. That's a seriously solid foundation to build on.

BALANCING ACT: TEN LIFE AREAS TO FOCUS ON FIRST

You may be wondering what you should focus on when you set aside your dedicated me time. After much research and conversation I've identified ten life balance areas that most benefit twentysomethings. To get you started, I've posted the best of the best resources by subject area on my Web site (www.myrealitycheckbounced.com).

1. **Conflict resolution.** On your path toward your Future Picture, you'll somehow get pulled into or start a conflict. These conflicts could happen at work, in relationships, with your family or elsewhere. Knowing how to resolve these conflicts benefits everyone involved, including you, and leads to a world with less pain and more peace. My friend Adam focused on this area and was finally able to reconnect with his dad after four years of not talking.

2. **Creativity.** You're making your mark on the world in a time of rapid change. To learn how to ask better questions and seek new solutions to old problems, develop your creativity. This mental muscle can be trained to become a major asset for your lifelong journey. For example, the more you practice solving tough real-world scenarios, the easier it will be for you to take over a team or organization in a time of extreme challenge, competition, or crisis.

3. **Financial literacy.** Social Security will not exist when you reach retirement age. If by some amazing chance it does, it probably won't support the lifestyle you want. To become financially free, you must educate yourself *early* on how to create your own personal balance sheet, cash flow statement, and investments. Time is on your side if you're wise enough to act *now* to create wealth *tomorrow*.

4. **Leadership.** Do you want to move up in your career, influence

your community, start your own business, or more actively shape your future? If so, you will benefit from developing your leadership skills. How will developing these skills speed up your success? These skills pull success to you by putting you in charge.

5. **Health and wellness.** As a human, your quality of life is directly linked to your lifestyle. Yes, you're living during a time of amazing health care and cutting-edge medicines. However, the most advanced medical treatments can't undo all the harm you can inflict on yourself. When it comes to your health and wellness, education and prevention are often the best medicines.

6. **International relations.** We share one planet, which constantly feels smaller thanks to such connectors as cell phones, influenza, pollution, and broadband. As more and more people share the same spinning ball of earth, we must learn to work as one team, not free agents with hidden agendas. Educating yourself about international relations can help you to play a role in global developments. Jen and Michael, two twenty-somethings living in Canada, were concerned about what was happening in the world, so they started a nonprofit Web site for young adults around the world to talk about global issues. Now over a million people a week log on to their site (www.takingitglobal.org) and share their comments.

7. **Motivation and resilience.** Life is going to throw curveballs and sucker punches at you no matter your background, education, or dreams. You must keep replenishing your energy by learning motivational teachings and techniques. The more inspired and resilient you become, the more likely you are to reach your Future Picture.

8. **Public speaking.** Talking in front of a large group of people is often touted as more terrifying than death. All the more reason to have excellent public speaking skills in your bag of real-

world tricks. Knowing how to effectively communicate your message to a room of decision makers can make the difference between your biggest setback and your biggest breakthrough.

9. **Problem solving.** In my interviews with executives and leaders, problem solving is the number one skill they look for in rising stars. Any employee can point to a problem, but only the most talented see the problem *and* offer solutions. Improving your problem-solving skills will help you solve the puzzles that trap your competition.

10. **Spirituality and purpose.** Everyone lives for a reason, and that reason is unique to each person. Your guiding purpose may be deeply religious, strongly spiritual, profoundly logical, or a combination of all three. Growing closer to this divining rod for your life brings greater peace and harmony to your journey. Rebecca set aside time every day to learn about different religions so she could find one that fit her. Three months later she feels more connected and at peace than ever before.

WHAT TIME IS IT IN YOUR WORLD?

Sara left her high-paying job because she realized that the corporate ladder she was racing up was just as fast wearing her down. Her new position as a high school teacher may not come with stock options and first-class travel, but she now wakes up excited to go to work—and how many people can honestly make the same claim?

I think many twentysomethings go through an overworked but underwhelmed crisis similar to Sara's. I know I did. We both learned the hard way that *being busy is not necessarily success.* When you're too busy you can't take time for yourself, so you miss out on what makes life so great. Once you do find your balance, you'll realize what it is you've been in such a rush to experience.

INSTANT MESSAGE

► Spare time is never found, it's always created.

► Where you focus your time reveals the true order of your priorities.

► All you need is thirty minutes a day to get on the right track.

BOUNCED: Being extremely busy means I'm a success.

CASHED: Success is having the time to do what makes me feel most alive.

ONLINE: Find out how Sara is doing at her new job at **www.myrealitycheckbounced.com/book**

11

CUTTING CORNERS

> If you can't tell your mama about it,
> you probably shouldn't be doing it.

REALITY-CHECK MOMENT:
SOMETIMES I HAVE TO COMPROMISE MY ETHICS TO GET AHEAD.

We are a short-attention-span generation. We see our peers make millions by the time they're twenty-five, and we want the same thing—*but* we don't want to have to wait for years or to work so hard to get it. We see politicians accepting bribes, pro athletes taking steroids, entertainers cheating on their wives and getting famous for it, and we think—am I missing the boat here? As a consequence, many of us are tempted to cut corners to get ahead quickly, even though we know it may be wrong.

The problem is that what may appear to be only a blurring of ethical lines to you can be a huge violation to others. Just one ill-conceived or ill-planned or ill-timed unethical choice can set you up for years of painful consequences that would otherwise have been *avoidable*. No matter what Future Picture you seek, if you pursue it with an unethical mind-set, you leave yourself wide open to potentially devastating and irreversible outcomes.

One glaring example of this is my friend Blake.* He was a young entrepreneur who started a business in his college dorm room about the same time I did. The major difference: My business was helping teens from tough backgrounds make better decisions. Blake's business was selling fake IDs (at least what I considered fake IDs) over the Internet. Here I was trying to reduce potentially painful paths such as underage drinking, college binge drinking, and drinking and driving, and Blake was getting rich enabling them.

Blake and I met, became friends, and had some serious talks about his business. He agreed to share his wild story in this book on the condition I tell it *from his perspective.* I think his story speaks to the unethical shortcuts we all will encounter:

Both my parents immigrated to the United States from Poland. Because we didn't have money, I was always looking for quick ways to make a buck. When I was about fifteen, I got my first real job. From the outside, my employer seemed to be running a normal business with a storefront, large sign, and lots of clients. But inside he sold "ID cards." These were very similar to state-issued driver's licenses, except they had a tiny disclaimer printed on the back: "For novelty use only."

The owner of the business was very successful. He had three houses, six cars, and retail stores in several cities. It was clear that what he was doing was somehow legal, because he'd been in business for ten years and wasn't hiding his services. After working for him a while, I figured I could make more if I could figure out how he was legally making these ID cards. I quit the job and hit the books.

After three months of research, I learned how my old boss

---

* Not his real name.

was creating these ID cards legally. It came down to exactly what was printed on the ID, how they were packaged, and a few other small but critical details. By knowing these details and strictly following the letter of the law, my old boss was able to stay in business by legally producing novelty IDs. About this time, the Internet was beginning to take off. I thought the Web might be the perfect way to sell my own ID cards.

AN ID IS BORN

By age seventeen, I knew how to legally design ID cards, how to build a good Web site, and how to operate a business. I went to college the next year ready to launch my ID card enterprise. What better place to launch this business than a college of fifty thousand students, about half of whom were underage?

I made ten sample ID cards, punched a hole in their corner, and put them on a metal ring. These were my display models. I then went dorm to dorm across the college peddling my ID cards. Wherever I went doors were slammed in my face, students told me I must be an undercover cop, and some said their buddy down the hall made better ones. I kept knocking.

My Web site went live one month later. The first week I got one order by mail. The next week I got ten. Two weeks after that I got forty Internet orders.

By the end of my first year in business, my little dorm-room ID card company had generated about $500,000 in sales! It was costing me around fifteen cents to make each card and I was selling them for $100 or more.

With such a profitable first year, I moved out of my dorm and into a fancy condo. I bought the biggest TV I could find, a huge saltwater aquarium, European leather couches, and the loudest stereo the electronics store had for sale. Life was amazing!

FROM BOOM TO DOOM

In my second year of business, my ID card company brought in almost $1,000,000 in sales! As rich as I was becoming, it was annoying having to constantly explain how what I was doing was not immoral, unethical, or illegal.

After two years of easy money and constant explanations, the discomfort I felt about the behaviors I might be enabling became overwhelming. What most ate at me was the idea of a minor using my ID card to buy alcohol, drive drunk, and then cause a car wreck that kills innocent people. I started thinking about closing the business all the time, but I was making thousands a week. Eventually, though, the money was worth less to me than having a clear conscience.

I was twenty years old. I had money. I could do what I wanted. I had invested in a start-up Internet venture and was excited about its potential. I had learned so much that I was ready to use. I decided to close my business on March 30, 1999.

But twenty days before I was going to close shop, I was out for coffee when I got a phone call from my neighbor. She told me that twelve federal agents had just busted down my front door with their guns drawn. She said it was like being in the TV show Cops.

The agents spent nine hours searching my condo. They took everything from my stereo speakers to the cash in my safe. I didn't know what to do, so I went to my lawyer's office. I sat on his couch scared out of my mind the entire day.

I had no idea if I was going to be arrested, interrogated, or what. All I knew was that I must be in big trouble. My lawyer learned that the FBI had a search warrant for my house but no arrest warrant for me—yet.

With my condo trashed, I stayed at my parents' house for two weeks. I'll never forget seeing so much pain in my parents' eyes. My selfish business decision was torturing them as much as me.

PUBLIC ENEMY NUMBER ONE

*Three months after the FBI raided my house, I learned that
the agents were part of a major investigation with a Senate
subcommittee in Washington, D.C. The focus was fake IDs and
the Internet. The subcommittee needed to make an example
out of someone to get support for changing the laws governing
ID cards. The same laws that I thought protected me. So they
chose to go after the biggest player in the entire U.S. novelty
card market—turns out that was me.*

*Their "make an example out of someone big" strategy
worked. Busting me made national news. Politicians watched
the news. They voted to change the laws.*

*Then I got an offer from the government. If I agreed to never
make ID cards again, they agreed not to prosecute me. It was
the fastest decision I ever made.*

It's been six years since I've held an ID card.

*Every day that I wake up and have the freedom to hang out
with my friends—or just to go to the bathroom when I want—
I am grateful for the lesson that came with losing my business.
I've decided that if I ever find myself having to persuade people
that something I'm involved in is ethically all right, then I
probably shouldn't be doing it. You might be able to talk
yourself into believing it's ethically okay, but you're taking a big
risk assuming that a jury of your peers will reach the same not
guilty conclusion.*

*I have to tell you, choosing an ethically solid path toward
your dreams may be much more difficult, but in the end it's a
lot less stressful and you don't have to hide it from your mom.*

In only two years Blake went from poor teenager to rich twentysomething to looking at serious jail time—all because he
blurred a seemingly obvious ethical line. He was lucky. He
ended up with a tarnished reputation and the loss of his toys,
but many people who followed in his footsteps have not been

so fortunate. Since the laws about IDs were changed based on Blake's business, people across the United States have earned long prison sentences trying to copy his early success.

SEPARATING RIGHT FROM WRONG

Some of you may read Blake's story and think that he did nothing wrong. He didn't force minors to buy his ID cards. They bought them of their own free will. And technically, he didn't even break the law. My question for people who defend his scheme is one of *intent*. If something is legal does that alone make it ethical? I don't think so.

If you were Blake, how would you justify *to your mom* taking money from thousands of minors so they could get a piece of plastic identifying them as older? Do you tell her they want to look older so they can get a better job—knowing their fake ID wouldn't pass a basic background check? Do you tell her they want to look older so they can defend their country— knowing that lying about your age to join the armed forces is a crime? When do you admit that you have to work really hard to convince your mom, let alone someone not related to you, that these ID card orders are not for a costume party?

Obviously none of these far-fetched scenarios would fly with any halfway rational mom. But Blake—or any reasonable adult for that matter—shouldn't need his mom to tell him what's right and what's wrong. At age twenty, he was old enough to know the difference. In his heart, Blake knew better. Maybe he chose not to see his business for what it was, but he couldn't blame that on his age or lack of worldly experiences—which he initially tried to do until his attorney explained it was a losing argument.

One of the harsh realities of being a twentysomething is that you no longer have your youthfulness to fall back on to excuse poor ethical choices. It didn't work for Blake and it won't work for you. If you're an adult and you commit a crime, you suffer adult-size consequences. There is no preferential treatment from a judge or jury whether you're forty-one or twenty-one. And there is no "Get Out of Jail Free" card because you got all A's in college and landed a good job. Twentysomethings who make ethically bad choices suffer consequences that can last a lifetime.

WHY WE CUT CORNERS

I know we all make mistakes. In fact, I've probably made *a lot more* mistakes than most. But ethically bad choices are different from mistakes. Mistakes come from a lack of preparation, information, experience, or pursuing the wrong opportunity. Ethically bad choices come from convincing yourself that *something you know is probably not right* is okay in your situation.

Maybe you or your friends have been caught making these unethical choices:

- Secretly hooking up with your best friend's boyfriend
- Not paying taxes on the cash tips you make waiting tables
- Lying to your parents about what you're studying in college
- Making a false insurance claim
- Listing fake jobs and accomplishments on your résumé

All of these unethical choices can be rationalized and justified if you try hard enough.

Amber, twenty-eight, knows this all too well. She received her first credit card soon after graduating college. She used it to buy clothes, food, and jewelry and quickly fell behind on the payments. When she finally maxed out that credit card she got another one. When that card maxed out she got another. She ran up over $40,000 in credit-card bills before she turned twenty-seven! When I asked her how she was going to pay off such huge credit-card debt, she replied, "I'm not going to pay it off. If the credit-card companies are stupid enough to keep sending me credit cards then I will keep using them. Then I'll just file bankruptcy and all the bills will go away." True to her word, she maxed out every credit card she could until she could not charge another cent. Then she filed for personal bankruptcy and her credit-card debt was erased. (*Warning*: The bankruptcy rules have since changed.)

Deep down, Amber knew this was wrong, but she did it anyway. Why? Most of the unethical choices we make, especially when it comes to getting ahead in the real world, come down to one reason: It's easier to bend the rules to get ahead than to take the high road, pay your dues, and possibly risk failure.

For this reason, it's *vital* you establish strong ethical standards early. Live up to them even if they push you onto a more difficult path. If you make a mistake but have solid ethics behind you, people will give you the benefit of the doubt. They'll encourage you to keep going, stay true to yourself and offer to help you move forward. When you make a mistake using poor ethics, people hope you forget their name and lose their number. Nobody wants a friend, spouse, or co-worker who can be trusted only half the time.

ETHICS 101

Regardless of your Future Picture, you're bound to encounter some unethical shortcuts that will help you get there faster. At these ethics crossroads, you can choose to take the unethical shortcut or keep to the high ground. Either way, you show your true colors in all their glory. You show them to yourself and to everyone else who will eventually find out about your decision.

With so much of your future riding on your ethical beliefs, it's important you are clear about what you stand for. Your ethics may be the only guiding light you have to navigate your darkest times. Take a moment and get your all-important definition of ethics in writing.

You define ethics as: _____

_____

I define ethics as separating right from wrong and then acting on what's right—*even if it's more difficult.*

What concerns me is that when I bring up the topic of ethics in conversations with twentysomethings, they usually go right to Enron, Martha Stewart, or a steroid-abusing athlete. They overlook the smaller, seemingly less important ethical decisions that they are faced with every day that can affect the rest of their lives.

These everyday decisions include keeping your promises, telling the truth, and treating people as you would like to be treated. You may think your ethical beliefs are not something you need to work on, because you always do the right thing *even when no one is looking.* This is totally possible, but I am confident you have a friend, family member, neighbor or co-worker who could use a little help in this area. Leading by example is the best way to help them see that ethics are the way to go if they want to go the distance.

WHAT WOULD YOU DO?

Consider how you would handle the following situations:

A. You find a wallet at a busy restaurant filled with money and credit cards.

B. You see a classmate cheating on a final exam that will be graded on a curve.

C. You are in charge of hiring and realize a hot prospect lied on his application.

D. You accidentally leave a grocery store without paying for a ninety-nine-cent item.

No two people will handle all four situations the same way. But how you respond to each situation says a lot about you. Would you try to contact the person who lost the wallet? Would you tell your professor about your cheating classmate? Would you confront the applicant who lied? Would you go back to the store and pay for the item?

You run across ethical dilemmas like these examples *every* day. Some are huge dilemmas with obvious consequences, Whereas others are small and might go unnoticed. Regardless of the size of your dilemmas, your ethics are the main compass you have to go by to consistently make the right decision. The more solid your ethics, the easier it will be for you to make the *right decisions* during your *toughest times* to reach the Future Picture you most desire.

Three years ago, a stranger made a seemingly small ethical decision that saved me a year's worth of late nights. I had left my laptop computer in the parking lot of a local coffee shop— Mozart's Coffee Roasters on Lake Austin. I was running late and talking on my cell phone and overlooked the fact I had put the computer down in the parking lot to unlock my car door. When I got home later that night I realized my computer was missing.

I mentally tried to retrace my steps. I remembered taking my computer out of the coffee shop, but I couldn't remember when I last saw it. As the hours passed I assumed it was lost for good.

Later that evening I got a call from an employee at Mozart's. He had found my computer in the parking lot and taken it inside the store in case someone came to claim it. When no one came for it by the end of his shift, he unzipped the front pocket of my laptop's bag, found my business card and called me.

I was so happy to have my computer back that I offered the employee a cash reward for his honesty. He turned it down, saying the money wasn't necessary, that returning the computer was simply *the right thing to do*. I'll never forget this employee's ethics. He didn't return my computer for praise, money or recognition. He returned it because *it was the right thing to do*. I now have every meeting I can at this coffee shop and even mentioned them in my book!

KARMA'N GET IT

As many ethical people as I've been lucky to meet in my travels, I've also encountered many a con man and con woman. Some of them even conned me! What continues to amaze me is how many of these frauds believed that they would forever get away with their schemes. They had convinced themselves that they were going to end up differently from the legions of con artists before them—who ultimately got caught and punished. It may take a while, but karma always catches up. And when poor ethical choices catch up to you, the consequences exceed the short-lived gains. Life has a funny way of cheating the biggest cheats.

Once you're labeled as unethical, it's a difficult stigma to change. I see this with Blake. He and I have stayed friends through the years, and I see how it frustrates him to always have to explain his former business whenever someone Googles his name.

The cruelest part of making unethical decisions is the way they can hurt those who love you the most. There have been many times when I've listened to an upset parent or spouse talk about how she's lost everything trying to keep a loved one out of jail. These compassionate people might as well have been the criminal, because they, too, were paying the price for the crime. Could you sleep at night if, as in one situation, your grandma was using her Social Security checks to pay for your criminal defense attorney?

BOUNCED: Ethics are nice in theory but not realistic if I want to get ahead in the real world.

CASHED: I should do what's right, even if *that's* the only reward.

FIVE QUESTIONS FOR MAKING TOUGH ETHICAL DECISIONS

Thanks to the recent corporate accounting scandals, government bribery scandals, and headline-grabbing celebrity affairs, ethics are playing an increasingly high-profile role in professional life. So how do you make sure you always make the right ethical decision? And will the right ethical decision always be clear, or is it sometimes as blurry as it seems?

To help you make tough ethical decisions, I've put together five questions that can provide guidance when you most need it. Answering these five questions will help you see that ethical choices aren't often as fuzzy as they sometimes appear.

1. Which outcome to the decision will allow you to sleep most peacefully one year from today?
2. Will anyone be hurt based on your decision, and does that person know he could be affected by your decision?
3. If your decision made newspaper headlines, would you be jeered or cheered?

4. Do you have to creatively justify your decision as ethical, and would strangers immediately agree with you?

5. If your mom and dad knew about your decision, would they be proud?

If you answer these five questions and are still unsure about what to do, it's time to get advice from those who care about you. Call your mentor and tag team for advice. Call your best friend. Call your religious leader. Call your mom. All these people know you, want what's best for you, and have survived their own ethical dilemmas. With their input, you'll be able to make the right ethical decision when it matters most.

WHAT ABOUT LITTLE WHITE LIES?

Calling for help may seem like an obvious choice when you're facing huge ethical dilemmas, but what if the decision doesn't feel important enough to deserve much thought? Maybe it's a tiny white lie explaining why you're late. Perhaps it's telling the electric company the check is in the mail when you know it isn't. If nobody gets hurt, are tiny unethical decisions bad?

In my experience, even the smallest white lie can take on a monstrous life of its own. You can find yourself lying on top of your previous lies just to stop the original lie from surfacing. Keeping a story of lies straight can be a real chore—and a needless one at that. If you'd just been honest in the first place, the other person probably would've forgotten about the whole thing. Instead, you're now on the hook big time.

Natt knows what it's like to turn a little white lie into a monstrous fake story. He decided to take a semester off from college but didn't want to tell his parents. They were paying for him to be there, and he knew they would stop sending money if he stopped going to class. So, he played along as if college were going great. Then he got comfortable not going to class, but he kept telling his parents college was going just fine. *This went on for three years.* At the end of it, he had to fake his own graduation—which included a fake diploma and transcript—and his parents threw him a graduation party! They didn't find out until a year later that his entire college career was a big fat lie.

Remember, *everyone* makes mistakes. When you make a mistake, apologize sincerely and move on. Telling a small lie only gives a tiny mistake the opportunity to become a big regret. People are willing to forgive you for being human, but they have long memories when it comes to liars, cheaters, thieves, and frauds.

FRIEND OR FAUX?

Maybe you have never fudged information on your résumé, lied to stay out of trouble, made a false insurance claim, shoplifted at the mall, or committed credit-card fraud. But you probably know someone who has. If you were both implicated in an ethical dilemma—say someone's Rolex turned up missing and you two were the only ones with keys to the apartment—do you think she would sell you out to save her own neck or would take the high road?

In trying to live an ethical existence, beware of your so-called friends who take pleasure reinforcing your poor decisions. I've seen this sabotage many talented twentysomethings. If your friends are unethical, it eventually rubs off on you. You may even think that if your buddies make the bad decision along with you that it can't be all that bad or that the punishment will be reduced. Wrong. *Bad ethical decisions lead to bad consequences.*

If you do find yourself making poor ethical choices only when certain friends are around, maybe it's time to hang out with some different people, the kind of people who actually want what's best for you rather than what's best for them.

Maria was caught in this situation at her job. She worked as a cashier at a busy pizza restaurant. The restaurant was primarily a cash business with lots of people coming and going at all hours. When she started work she quickly found out that the cashiers she worked with would steal $20 from their register after each shift. They told her she should do the same, because they all were underpaid and "in this together." After a month she gave in and started taking $20 after each shift. She justified it by telling herself that her co-workers were doing it, too. The owner finally got wind that someone was stealing from his restaurant, so he secretly installed a videocamera above the cash registers. With this evidence he immediately fired all the cashiers including Maria. The other cashiers then tried to explain their actions by saying it was Maria's idea all along, and that they were just going along with her.

ETHICS RULE!

Between the time you first opened this book and the time you finish reading it, you'll have made *many* decisions based on your ethics. Maybe you kept a promise to a friend. Maybe you told a tiny white lie to your boss. Maybe you returned a lost item. All of these choices represent your everyday ethics.

When you live with solid ethics, people won't think twice about trusting you at their weakest moments, asking you to join their team, or sharing with you their most personal secrets. But once you prove your ethics are spotty, people pay attention and *never forget*.

When you live by a high ethical standard your word *is* your bond. People know they can count on you in the good times and the bad. Plus, when a potential love interest or employer

Googles your name, they'll find more reasons to trust you—not bad press. And you won't have to hide what you are doing from your mom!

INSTANT MESSAGE

► Separate right from wrong and then do what's right, even if it's more difficult.

► One tiny lie can lead to a tangle of false stories.

► When you stand up for what's right, you'll always be on firm ground.

BOUNCED: Ethics are nice in theory but not realistic if I want to get ahead in the real world.

CASHED: I should do what's right, even if *that's* the only reward.

ONLINE: For more info on Blake's wild story, visit **www.myrealitycheckbounced.com/book**

12

FIND OUT WHAT YOU'RE MADE OF

> To feel alive, start living!

We all come to a certain point in our lives, usually in our twenties, when our careers start to become established, some big life choices have already been made, and a familiar routine begins to take hold. And yet there's still a feeling of unease; a feeling of subtle second-guessing. You begin to wonder: Did I make the right choices? Am I stuck in a comfort zone that keeps me from seizing the day? How do I know if I'm headed down the right path? How do I know if this is the best I can do with what I have? How do I know for certain if I am living life to the fullest? In short—Is this all there is? Asking these questions simply proves you want *the most* you can get out of your life; and luckily, there is one answer to all of them: Start living in the moment.

You don't have to keep telling yourself that *one day* you're going to lose weight. Join a health club or take up hiking *right now*. You don't have to settle on one career path just because that's what your college degree was or because you've been doing it for a few years. Take a chance and explore other opportunities. If you can't see those opportunities, go create them! You don't have to punch a clock every day if your most inspiring dream is to travel the world. Go do it now. Just because a path worked for other people, doesn't mean it is the right path for you. Your authentic path is exactly that—yours.

Mysha, twenty-three, understands how difficult it can be to find the path that feels completely right. She had dreamed since she was a kid about becoming a traditional middle school teacher, until her reality check bounced. During her first real teaching experience—student teaching in her last year of college—she was assigned to work in an affluent suburban middle school. She quickly realized that working in such a mundane environment did not deeply inspire her. In fact, the only time she felt in the moment was when she was helping the kids other teachers had written off as beyond help. She gave this feedback to the dean of her college and asked to be transferred to a school with more at-risk students. The dean didn't like Mysha challenging his placement of her, so he transferred her to an even more affluent school and assigned her to kindergarteners! She quit the College of Education in protest—as a senior.

Mysha was forced to graduate with a different degree from the one she intended, but she was not going to quit just because her reality check bounced costing her her teaching certification. Instead, she decided to pave her own path to help those who most inspired her. Stepping *way* out of her comfort zone—and going down an all-new path—Mysha joined Teach for America (TFA). This program places recent college graduates in two-year teaching assignments at the neediest U.S. public schools. Mysha, a six-foot-tall brunette born and raised in the suburbs, was assigned to South Central Los Angeles.

FINDING HER WAY

Mysha arrived for her first day of work at a gang-infested middle school that straddles the border between Watts and South Central. About two thousand students in grades six to eight attended the school. The neighboring high school graduated roughly 50 percent of its students—and those were the ones who stayed in school long enough to actually start ninth grade.

Mysha was immediately taken aback by the students at her new middle school. They have seen it all. Many feel angry, hopeless, and victimized. They have gone to sleep with the sounds of gunfire and gangland chaos for so long they can't imagine it any other way. Mysha was making a big leap of faith in herself by believing she had anything to offer them. And then she learned she was assigned to the neediest students on the campus: the special education students.

It took Mysha one frustrating week just to locate her thirty special education students. In the meantime, she got an eye-opening introduction to South Central: Kids beating up kids, parents threatening teachers, teachers being punched by students. It was so wild that surrounding neighborhoods had drive-by shootings *in the middle of the afternoon*. Mysha was in shock that first week, but with each passing day she felt more and more alive, determined, confident, and inspired.

Mysha tried every creative way she could to teach her students. It was slow going. These students were trying to survive in South Central while struggling with disabilities from autism to dyslexia. Even though Mysha's students initially saw her only as "just another white teacher trying to save the world through their school," she had an advantage in empathizing with her students' situation. Mysha has muscular dystrophy. Even in her mild case, she knows what a difference a little patience, love, and hope can make.

The low point of that first year jarred Mysha back into the reality of the path she was paving. She went to break up a fight in which a student was punching a teacher in the face. The hallway was crowded with kids cheering and yelling. Mysha broke through the crowd to pull the student off the teacher, but then the student turned around and attacked *her*. When the police finally arrived Mysha was bleeding—physically, emotionally, and spiritually. As wounded as she felt, she also knew that she was in the right place to make the biggest difference possible. That feeling of purpose was something she would never forget.

BOUNCED: There has to be more to life than this.

CASHED: By opening myself up to different possibilities and a more authentic path, I can experience more meaning than I ever dreamed possible.

I asked Mysha why she teaches in South Central. I wondered why she put her life on the line when she could work in so many other less physically, emotionally, and spiritually challenging schools. She gave this example as an explanation:

At the beginning of the school year, my kids hated after-school tutoring. They refused to bring their textbooks, homework, or supplies. Last week, with the school year winding down, I left my classroom to talk with a teacher across the hall. When I got back the students were arguing loudly. I settled them down and asked them to explain what they were yelling about. It turns out they were arguing over how to solve a math word problem! In disbelief, I offered to help, but they said, "No Ms W. We can figure this out. You made us smart enough."

Mysha, or—as her students refer to her—"Ms W," found her authentic path in the world by going in a direction that she knew would test her to her limits. *But that was what she needed to find out what she was made of.* Sure, at times she was scared, frustrated, and insecure; but better to face those fears and feel alive than play it safe and never know the reward of living in the moment.

SPREAD YOUR WINGS AND START FLYING

You don't have to go to work in South Central to find out what your life is all about. That was Mysha's answer to the question. What you do have to know is that life rarely goes exactly as planned. There will always be unexpected challenges with good and bad outcomes. But it is seizing those moments of highs and lows that make your heart race, your spirit soar, each day count, and your grandkids sit up in their seats at dinner when you tell them your life story!

Whatever path you choose to start living like you mean it— whether that's joining the Peace Corps in Africa, taking an entry-level sales job, getting a master's degree in molecular biology, or starting your own denim boutique—you have to invest yourself 100 percent. If you don't jump into life with both feet, you never get the satisfaction, thrill, and lessons that are waiting to be discovered. You will know you're on the right path when you willingly do the most menial, repetitive work necessary to make progress, because you know it's moving you closer to where you are inspired to be.

You don't get out of your life what you are given. *You get out of your life what you do with it.*

MAKE THE CHOICE TO FEEL ALIVE

When you choose to keep learning, growing, testing yourself, and evolving, you are on a course that leads to your highest state of being. This commitment to applying yourself day after day, month after month, year after year is certainly not the path of least resistance but it certainly is the most rewarding. When you choose to live on terms you dictate, you add greater meaning to every waking moment. You set in motion a chain of events leading to the Future Picture you created in the beginning of this book.

No matter where you are starting from:

1. You choose where you go from here.
2. You can change direction as many times as you need.
3. You will find what makes you feel most alive *when you start living in the moment!*

These three facts make this period in your life so incredibly exciting—and sometimes overwhelming. The key is to not lose sight of *your power* to make your life more the way you want every day. This is your time. Courageously seek to discover who you are, what makes you excited to be alive, and when you most savor every breath. You have an inspiring Future Picture. Pour yourself into making it your present, and you will know you're living to the fullest.

SCHOOL OF HARD KNOCKS

Sometimes going out on a limb to feel most alive will work out exactly the way you want, sometimes it won't. Remember there is no such thing as happily ever after in the real world. All you have to work with is right now. Life will always present obstacles, risks, and skeptics. Sometimes these will cause you to throw up and other times they will cause you to show up. The key is to not doubt yourself and your Future Picture. A beautiful life is ahead of you, if you are willing to keep moving along a path toward what's authentically right *for you right now*.

And, believe me, the rewards are well worth the sometimes scary journey. As Anita, age twenty-eight, can tell you, the bigger the risks you take toward your Future Picture, the more alive you begin to feel.

I've always liked doing things on my own terms and being in control of my future, so I went to college a year early. I graduated at nineteen with a degree in management information systems. I took a well-paying job with a large technology company and jumped into the real world.

Looking back I can now see that I did all that because I felt like it was what I was supposed to do. *I was* supposed *to go to college. I was* supposed *get a good job. I was* supposed *to settle down. But after six months at that first job, I wasn't happy. That wasn't* supposed *to happen.*

So, I decided to find out what would make me happy. I quit the job. Then I persuaded my parents to let me run a small Montessori school they owned while I went back to school at night.

The longer I worked for my parents, the more I felt the pull toward taking on a big, defining challenge. The only thing I could think of that got me excited was the idea of starting my own Montessori school. I had dreamed about it since I was a kid, but I was beginning to see it was now or never. I chose now.

I began driving around town looking for land that fit the school I imagined opening. One day I stumbled on to the perfect place. The next day I went to the bank, showed them my business plan and took the biggest, craziest, most outrageous risk of my twenty-year-old life: I pledged my entire trust fund against the loan I would need to start the school.

That may sound simple, but when your parents work their whole lives to leave you money so you won't have to work as hard as they did, betting it all on an unproven business idea is scary—especially when you're twenty. I was essentially betting my safe and secure future on a totally unproven vision in my mind!

I remember sitting at the bank and feeling all the stares as I was handed a check for a little over $1,000,000. I know they were thinking, "What are we doing?" or "What is she doing:" At that moment, I knew I had no choice but to somehow make it work.

From that day forward, I didn't stop, pause, or slow down. I ran my parent's Montessori school during the day, worked on my master's degree at night, and started my own Montessori school in the time in between. As overwhelmed as I was, I'd never felt more alive.

I finished my master's degree about the time we broke ground on my school. I remember spending every day in a little room at a nearby community center making my presentation to parents about why they should trust me with their children's education. It was intense. My credibility—and age—was challenged every day.

As this was going on, the general contractor building the school of my dreams filed for bankruptcy. He went bankrupt two months before the school was supposed to open! Here I was, trying to persuade parents to give me a $500 deposit to hold a space for their kid, and suddenly, all construction on my new school stopped. I ended up being forced to finish building the school backward; the carpet was installed before the ceilings.

The worst part of the construction delay was that I would have to open the school two months late. This put me in a horrible position. I had to tell all the parents who had placed their faith—and their child's future—in my hands that their kid would have to start school late. I remember being woken up every morning to my cell phone ringing with an angry parent on the line. It was miserable, but the experience only built my resolve to make the school a success.

In September, two full months behind schedule, I finally opened Starwood Montessori School. I had hoped a hundred kids ages two to nine would enroll. Miraculously, almost two hundred students enrolled by the end of the first year. In our second year, we reached our max capacity of three hundred students. Now we are one of the largest schools in our area— and I'm breaking ground on another school next year!

It may sound crazy, but after all the ups, downs, and unknowns I went through to live my dream, I'd definitely do it all over again the same way. The stress, uncertainty, upset parents, and leaps of faith only make me appreciate more when my students run up to me with a big hug and say "Good morning, Ms Anita!"

I know now that I'm living my purpose. That's a wonderful feeling.

By taking the risk to follow her heart and by betting everything she had on that path, Anita found a zest for life that many people only dream about. Her courage in following her authentic path is rewarded every morning when her students show up with smiles, hugs, and handwritten thank-you notes.

NOW IT'S YOUR TIME

You may be thinking your situation is different from Anita's or Mysha's. Maybe you are younger or older. Maybe your biggest dream is not that big or it's so big you're afraid to start. These are all the more reasons to begin proving to yourself what you are made of right *now*. With each baby step and giant leap you take toward feeling most alive, you move farther down a path leading to the inspiration, reward, and purpose you desire.

To remind you where you're headed, take a moment to write your four snapshots in the following lines. Feel free to revise them from the ones you wrote at the beginning of the book. Next to each snapshot write one step—tiny or huge—that you are willing to commit to taking *this week*. With each step you take, you'll have a better idea of where to go to feel more alive.

Career snapshot: _____

- Sample action: Call someone who has your dream job and take her to lunch. Find out what it's really like to do what she does—and if she can help you to do the same.
- Your action: _____

Family snapshot: _____

- Sample action: Organize a family reunion.
- Your action: _____

Personal snapshot: _____

- Sample action: Join a health and wellness group such as yoga, meditation, dance, or spin classes.
- Your action: _____

Purpose snapshot: _____

- Sample action: Write your purpose snapshot on your bathroom mirror.
- Your action: _____

SHARE YOUR KNOWLEDGE, GRASSHOPPER

As all the stories in this book reveal, you have so many exciting options about what to do with the rest of your life. Along with focusing on your wide-open future, it's important to remember the choices that have moved you to where you are now. I'm positive that if you reflect on your biggest watershed moments—such as deciding whether to continue your education, whether to get a new job, whether to ask your best friend to marry you—there were other people involved in helping you make the right decision. Without these advisers' help, guidance, and belief, you might not be where you are now. These important people may have been family, friends, teachers, employers, your tag team, or a mentor. The best way you can thank them is to share what you've learned with other people not as far along their path as you are. You do this by becoming a mentor yourself.

You may think that you don't know enough to mentor someone else, but you absolutely do! By making it this far in life, you've picked up lots of knowledge, ideas, and experiences *the hard way* that other people could benefit from learning. Becoming a mentor doesn't mean you're expected to have all the answers to every problem, or write someone into your will—all it means is that *you help someone the best you know how.* You might end up saving this person from falling on his face or you will be there to help him get up when he does fall, and all the while you reinforce his belief that one day he, too, can make something meaningful of his life.

For you to truly master all that you've learned, *you must share it with someone else.*

Here's how to spread your wisdom by becoming a mentor:

1. **Know what you know.** Identify what you're good at that others might want to learn. Consider aspects of your life in which

you've succeeded, such as living on your own, overcoming tough stuff, graduating from school, working with diverse people, leading a team, or moving to a new city. You aren't expected to know it all, only enough to help someone less experienced or less confident make it through the confusion.

2. **Open yourself to mentoring someone younger or older.** The saying "The teacher will appear when the student is ready" is accurate. Be wise enough to notice when someone you could help is ready for your assistance. You can speed up this connection by joining an organization like Big Brothers Big Sisters, volunteering with groups that promote mentoring (such as Junior Achievement), or by visiting a local school and signing up as a mentor. If you want to help someone older, volunteer at a nursing home or community center that serves the elderly. Someone is waiting *right now* for you to help her make her life a little better.

3. **Take it slowly.** You don't have to magically fix your mentee's home life or solve all his financial problems overnight. Most people, regardless of age and accomplishments, simply want someone to genuinely listen. If he needs advice he'll ask for it. You know how confusing life can get. At those toughest moments, most of us just want someone to listen and remind us that it will be okay. Knowing that you care about your mentee is often more meaningful to him than any advice you can share.

4. **Grow with them.** As you get to know your mentee, identify one or two areas that you both agree are most important to focus on. These could include school, ethics, work, leadership, relationships, health, or spirituality. Recommend books, give her challenges, and help her learn the lessons she will need to know to get where she wants to go.

If you're still sitting there wondering "When am I going to use all this information?" or "When should I get started?" then it's time you answer your own question by acting on your biggest dreams *immediately*. No matter how far away your Future Picture may seem, it will move closer as soon as you take action to reach for it. The difference you make by applying your education in your own life and the lives of others is your *real-world report card*.

OKAY IS NOT GOOD ENOUGH!

There is no doubt Mysha could have become a teacher at a calm, suburban school, but *she wanted more*. She wanted to make a difference and feel alive in the process. There is no doubt that Anita, too, could have made a good living working at the tech company, but *she also wanted more*. She wanted to run her own school and take control of her future. There is no doubt that you could settle down along your current path and be okay, but *you also want more*.

Why do you want more out of your life? Because on some level you know that okay is not good enough!

Okay is not challenging or meaningful. Okay is not making the most of your talents, dreams, abilities, and creativity. Okay is doing the minimum *and getting the minimum in return*. Okay was not good enough for Mysha or Anita, and it absolutely should not be good enough for you—*and you know it!*

How many times have you thought, "If I don't do this now, I may never do it." The question is whether you are going to act on it. Time is passing by whether you choose to make the most of it or not. It's your choice. Choose to make the most of what you have by refusing to settle for okay and instead following your Future Picture wherever it leads, whether that is South Central Los Angeles or Mount Everest.

MAKE YOUR FUTURE PICTURE YOUR PRESENT PICTURE

Imagine how fantastic it will feel to wake up and know that you are spending your day doing exactly what you believe you were born to do. *You can*. All you have to do is take what you have learned in this book and apply that know-how starting today; then stick with it until you create the life you want.

Only you can make the decisions and take the actions necessary to get more out of your life. If you're not thrilled where you are, then it's time to get a move on! *You have the power*.

Think about it this way, with each step you take toward your Future Picture:

- You forever change your view of yourself and your world.
- You separate what you like from what you don't.
- You prove what you can accomplish.
- You learn expensive lessons you can't buy.
- You unravel clues to why you're on this planet.
- You find paths to the people you need.
- You move nearer your purpose.
- You show you're not helpless or a victim.
- You inch closer and closer to finding out what you are truly made of.
- You build your confidence and write your future.

THE SKY IS NO LONGER THE LIMIT

After graduating college, Joby was in a position familiar to anyone whose reality check has bounced. He knew in his mind and in his heart that there had to be a more meaningful path than the one he was on. He had tried grad school, but that only left him with debt, a degree, and little direction. He had a high-paying desk job, but that just filled his wallet while draining his spirit. He needed a challenge, a goal, a purpose—something so outrageous it would test him to the core of his very being.

So he started exercising, working odd jobs to save money, and taking out loans. When he thought he was ready, he took his biggest leap of faith ever. He sold everything he could live without and bought a plane ticket to the Himalayas. This seemed as far as a twenty-four-year-old from Louisiana could travel, but sometimes you have to go to the other side of the world to find what's missing inside of you.

Joby spent five weeks at Base Camp below Mount Everest while his body adjusted to the harsh climate and high altitude. He knew what he was about to do would test him, because it had *killed* several of his friends the year before. The obvious danger only fueled his passion.

On the designated day, Joby packed his climbing gear and supplies and started up the mountain. For five days he climbed through snow, ice, and freezing wind. The weather was so rough that halfway up the mountain everyone else in his climbing group turned back. They were all older than him and wise enough to not go any farther. Joby just kept climbing skyward.

On the fifth day he could see the summit. It was still dark but the snow was so white it glowed against the deep blue of the sky. At this altitude, Joby was the highest person on the face of the earth. He reached the summit of Mount Everest almost one year to the day when he made the soul-searching decision to find out what he was really made of. Watching the sun part the horizon and dance across the rigid peaks, Joby felt more alive than ever before in his twenty-four years. It was a moment that he says stays with you.

For an hour, Joby stood 29,028 feet above sea level and watched the world show off. He returned to the United States a changed person. Not only was he the youngest American to ever summit Mount Everest—and an unknown climber at that—but he had climbed onto the path of his calling: He wanted to share the mountains with people who would never be able to physically scale their peaks. His brainstorm idea was to start a film company devoted to bringing the most remote mountains into people's living rooms.

By recognizing that he wanted more out of his life and then acting to quench that restlessness, Joby went from a confined cubicle in Louisiana to the expansive heights of the Himalayas to running a film company headquartered in Italy. Did it work out exactly the way he planned? No. Was he ever scared, frustrated, and unsure? Yes. Does he credit the experience with making him feel more alive than ever before? Absolutely.

By seeking to find out what he was made of, Joby found instead what he had been missing: his passion for life. He took his bounced reality check and turned it into a windfall of purpose.

IS THIS IT?

Wherever you find yourself on your path to living with passion and meaning, just remember that you, *and only you*, choose how you live your life. You can settle for safe, uninspired existence, and continue to let your reality check bounce, or you can rise to the challenge by making your life as grand as you imagine.

In Chapter 1, Tiffany asked with frustration "Is *this* it?" What she didn't know was that she had the answer all along—even the right words, just the wrong order. Stop asking yourself "Is *this* it?" and start proclaiming "*This* is *it*!" Together let's make the most of it!

INSTANT MESSAGE

► Take the path that feels most right for you—even if it's unproven.

► Thank those who helped you by becoming a mentor to someone who needs you.

► You get to live your life on *your terms*. Choose to rise to the occasion!

BOUNCED: There has to be more to life than this.

CASHED: Today is my opportunity to start making my life exactly the way I want it to be.

ONLINE: Read more about Mysha, Anita, and Joby at **www.myrealitycheckbounced.com/book**

SUGGESTED RESOURCES

Twenty-one Books to Inspire Twentysomethings
1. *How to Win Friends and Influence People*, Dale Carnegie (Pocket Books, 1998. Orig. pub. 1936.)
2. *It's Not About the Bike*, Lance Armstrong with Sally Jenkins (G. P. Putnam's Sons, 2000.)
3. *Jonathan Livingston Seagull*, Richard Bach (Scribner, 2006. Orig. pub. 1970.)
4. *Man's Search for Meaning*, Viktor E. Frankl (Washington Square Press, 1985. Orig. pub. 1946.)
5. *Quarterlife Crisis*, Alexandra Robbins and Abby Wilner (Jeremy P. Tarcher/Putnam, 2001.)
6. *The Seven Habits of Highly Effective People*, Stephen R. Covey (Simon & Schuster, 1989.)
7. *Rich Dad, Poor Dad*, Robert T. Kiyosaki with Sharon L. Lechter, C.P.A. (Warner Business Books, 2000.)
8. *The Alchemist*, Paolo Coelho (HarperSanFrancisco, 2006. Orig. pub. 1988.)
9. *The E-Myth Revisited*, Michael E. Gerber (HarperCollins, 1995.)
10. *The Four Agreements*, Don Miguel Ruiz (Amber-Allen Publishing, 1997.)
11. *The Greatest Salesman in the World*, Og Mandino (Bantam, 1985. Orig. pub. 1968.)
12. *The Instant Millionaire*, Mark Fisher (New World Library, 1990.)
13. *The Little Engine That Could*, Watty Piper (Grosset & Dunlap, 1978. Orig. pub. 1930.)

14. *The Little Red Book of Selling*, Jeffrey Gitomer (Bard Press, 2004)
15. *The Richest Man in Babylon*, George S. Clason (Signet, 1988. Orig. pub. 1926.)
16. *The Road Less Traveled*, M. Scott Peck, M.D. (Touchstone, 2003. Orig. pub. 1978.)
17. *The Success Principles*, Jack Canfield with Janet Switzer (HarperCollins, 2005.)
18. *The World is Flat*, Thomas L. Friedman (Farrar, Straus & Giroux, 2005.)
19. *Think and Grow Rich*, Napoleon Hill (Ballantine, 1987. Orig. pub. 1937.)
20. *Unlimited Power*, Anthony Robbins (Fireside, 1997. Orig. pub. 1986.)
21. *What Should I Do With My Life?*, Po Bronson (Random House, 2002.)

Fourteen Organizations to Consider Joining

Big Brothers Big Sisters	www.bbbs.org
Entrepreneurs' Organization	www.eonetwork.org
Global Youth Action Network	www.youthlink.org
Habitat for Humanity	www.habitat.org
Junior Achievement	www.ja.org
Kiwanis International	www.kiwanis.org
The National Foundation for Teaching Entrepreneurship	www.nfte.com
Points of Light Foundation	www.pointsoflight.org
Rotary International	www.rotary.org
TakingITGlobal.org	www.takingitglobal.org
Teach for America	www.teachforamerica.com
Toastmasters International	www.toastmasters.org
US Chamber of Commerce	www.uschamber.com
Your industry's professional association	

READER DISCUSSION GUIDE

When your reality check bounces, it's important to know you are not alone in your journey to get back on track. Use the following questions to talk through your experience with friends, family, or other trusted advisors so you can start to create the life you want.

1. At what moment did you realize your reality check had bounced? How did you know? How did you initially deal with this unsettling realization? Who did you tell first? Why?

2. Which story in the book most connects with you? Why? What insight did you gain from reading this story? If you were to write your own story, how would it be similar to and different from the one that most connected with you?

3. Have you ever been in a situation, like Josh in Chapter 2, in which you were forced to start over from scratch in a new place? Were you scared? Why did you go through with it? What was the biggest lesson your learned? Looking back, do you believe this experience of starting over in a new setting made you stronger?

4. When you imagine the future you want to create, what aspect most excites you? Why? What are you doing this week to move closer to your Future Picture? How are you daily reminding yourself of the future you have the power to create?

5. We all face obstacles in our quest to live our authentic dreams. What is the biggest real-world obstacle you transformed into a breakthrough opportunity? How can you apply your learning from this experience to other areas in your life?

6. Jerry, in Chapter 5, was described as the "Mayor of the Four Seasons" for his relentless networking. Do you know someone like Jerry? Where are they most successful at making quality contacts? When was the last time you went to an event with the goal of expanding your network? What group or organization could you join that would help you meet the people necessary to reaching your dreams? What is your best Introductory Message?

7. Finding a mentor helped Jimmy, in Chapter 6, to live his most inspiring dreams. Do you have a mentor or mentors? If so, how did you get them? What do you seek to learn from them? How has having a mentor made you a better person? If you don't have a mentor, what would it take for you to actively seek one?

8. Almost everyone has experienced trauma in their past. In Chapter 7, Lindsay had to confront trauma in her past to free herself to reach for her dreams. What is the most traumatic experience in your past? Have you come to terms with this difficult experience, or is it still lingering in the back of your mind? Who can help you deal with this painful experience so you can move on with your life?

9. Sean, in Chapter 8, was born with bones so fragile they can break if he shakes hands. In spite of this ready-made excuse, he went on to graduate from college, write a book, and create an exercise video! What excuse most keeps you in your

comfort zone? Why is this excuse so effective in sabotaging your courage and motivation? What would it take for you to let go of this excuse?

10. Fear is a universal human emotion. What is your biggest fear? How does this fear surface in your life? What could you do this week that would position you to face this fear and emerge stronger than ever?

11. What is the toughest ethical decision you have ever been forced to make? Would you make the same decision again? Are your ethics the same as they were ten years ago? How are they different?

12. What is the biggest risk you've ever taken to reach your Future Picture? How did you feel when you took the risk? What did you learn from the experience? Would you do it again?

13. Pursuing your authentic dreams positions you to create an inspiring legacy. What do you want your legacy to say? What could you do to strengthen your legacy?

Post your own discussion questions at www.myrealitycheckbounced.com/inside.

ACKNOWLEDGMENTS

Writing this book took two years. I had no idea it would be such an endeavor. I thought I would simply escape to a cozy coffee shop for a few months and capture my thoughts, stories, ideas, and observations. I was wrong. My solitary writing journey became just the opposite. I spent almost the entire two years living out of a suitcase to get a firsthand perspective on my generation's coming-of-age experience. This nonstop flying, driving, scheduling, calling, interviewing, e-mailing, writing, and revising was made possible by an amazing team of people ready to help me at every turn—and occasional U-turn!

I owe the biggest thanks to Kris Puopolo, my brilliant editor at Broadway. Kris championed this book from the very beginning and never wavered. Kris: Thank you for believing in me and the importance of my message.

A special thank-you goes to Jonathan Small, my creative editing resource. Jonathan: Thanks for taking 100 of my words and making them 10! I also must recognize my former professor and dear friend Elota Patton. Thanks for pulling my abstract ideas into one cohesive process. You rock!

I also extend a heartfelt thank-you to my literary agent, Jan Miller at Dupree Miller in Dallas. I walked in off the street and you put me on a plane to New York City.

To the key people I rely on every day to pursue my mission: Sondra, thanks for sticking with me no matter the time zone or obstacle. Remember when I wasn't old enough to rent a car? Look how far we've come! I couldn't do it without you. To Denise, the love of my life, thanks for being my inspiration, best friend, dance partner, and fiancée. You add meaning to my every moment.

To my family: I wouldn't be here if you hadn't encouraged me to chase my dreams, even when they seemed totally unrealistic. Thanks for your love, candid feedback, and constant support. I look forward to our next vacation adventure! Special thanks go to Alanna DeSimio (you go, Sis!), Mom, Dad, John, Randy, Amy, David, and Grandpa.

I owe a HUGE thanks to the people who selflessly allowed me to share their stories in this book. You know who you are. Thanks for trusting me to share something so personal. Your stories make this book powerful.

Finally, I'd like to thank the mentors, advisors, and friends who have been with me every step of the way: Admiral Bob Inman, Angelos Angelou, Adan Armandariz, Alan Blake, Ben Quinto, Bill Miller, Bob Carlquist, Brad Duggan, Chris Weaver, Corey Yulinsky, Damon Brown, Dan Akers, Dr. Kosmetsky, Fred Akers, Jack Canfield, Jay Mechling, Jerry Harris, Jerry Morgan, Jim Vidak, Jimmy Ardoin, Joe Machemehl, Jordan Bean, Josh Solomon, Keith Price, Kenan Thompson, Kyle Frazier, Lisa King, Lou Cinquino, Lowell Leberman, Mark Meussner, Mark Strama, Michael Tashnick, Mike Sheridan, Orlando, Walt Tashnick, Pat Giddis, Patrick Boylan, Peter Laird, Peter Rosenstein, Peter Yarrow, Richard Williams, Richard Wong, Ron Johnson, Scott Friedman, Shelby Carter, Stephen Shang, Teresa Esparza, Tiffany Webb, Tom Segesta, Travis Doss, Woody Frasier, and Zack Lynde.

About the Author

JASON RYAN DORSEY authored his first bestselling book at age eighteen. Since that time, he has spoken to more than 500,000 people around the world. Jason's books have been used in about 1,500 colleges, schools, corporations, and workforce development programs. He has been featured on NBC's *Today Show* and ABC's *The View*. To learn more about Jason, visit **www.jasondorsey.com** or **www.myrealitycheckbounced.com**.

Jason Ryan

Bring Jason's Powerful Message to Your College, Conference or Corporation

Jason Dorsey knows how to inspire an audience! In the last ten years, he has delivered more than one thousand speeches to audiences across the United States and as far away as Egypt, Spain, Finland, and India. Jason has taught corporate executives how to build loyalty with young professionals. He's helped young professionals get promoted faster and has shown college students of all backgrounds how to land (or create) their dream jobs. Jason's programs are popular because he blends wildly entertaining stories with specific actions you can take immediately.

Jason's Most Popular Corporate and Conference Talks:

Outgrow Your Cubicle™: Create more value for your company and get rewarded!
Loyalty @ Any Age: How to connect generations in the workplace so everyone wins.
You Must Be Present to Win™: Make every day an opportunity.

Jason's Most Popular College Talks:

My Reality Check Bounced!: How to cash in on your real-world dreams
College Is Not a Career: Make the most of the college experience.
Leadership Is a Lifestyle: Learn it, live it, love it!

To check Jason's availability—and to receive his free informational DVD— please visit www.jasondorsey.com or www.myrealitycheckbounced.com.

Dorsey

Want Instant Opportunities to Cash Your Reality Check?

Visit www.myrealitycheckbounced.com to access TONS of free online resources, get your real-world questions answered by Jason, and connect with other people trying to find their authentic life path.

On the website you can:

- Find additional information about the people whose stories are shared in the book
- Locate free resources that coincide with each book chapter
- E-mail questions directly to Jason
- Win free stuff by signing up for Jason's sometimes outrageous but always entertaining newsletter
- Download a bonus book chapter for FREE!